THIS LIFE ON EARTH

This Life on Earth

edited by Dinah Livingstone

Sea of Faith (SOF) Network
Britain

2nd edition August 2009.
First published on 22nd July 2009,
Mary Magdalene's Day,
by Sea of Faith (SOF) Network,
3 Belle Grove Place,
Spital Tongues,
Newcastle upon Tyne NE2 4LH
www.sofn.org.uk
© Copyright remains with the authors 2009.

The front cover picture is *Sunset and Moonrise*, a pastel drawing by Tom Livingstone. The back cover picture is *Glad Day* by William Blake. Designed and typeset in-house mainly in 12 point Garamond. Printed in England by imprint**digital**.net

ISBN: 978-0-9523930-8-5

British Library Cataloguing in Publication Data:
A catalogue record for this book is available from the British Library.

Foreword by William Blake

The Marriage of Heaven and Hell, Plate 11

The ancient Poets animated all sensible objects with Gods or Geniuses, calling them by the names and adorning them with the properties of woods, rivers, mountains, lakes, cities, nations, and whatever their enlarged and numerous senses could perceive.

And particularly they studied the genius of each city and country, placing it under its mental deity;

Till a system was formed, which some took advantage of, and enslaved the vulgar by attempting to realise or abstract the mental deities from their objects: thus began Priesthood;

Choosing forms of worship from poetic tales.

And at length they pronounced that the Gods had ordered such things.

Thus men forgot that All deities reside in the human breast.

Contents

FOREWORD BY WILLIAM BLAKE

INTRODUCTION   1

PROSE
Don Cupitt: *Changes and Chances*   5
John Pearson: *No Safe Comforts*   9
Cicely Herbert: *It Belongs to Us All*   17
Tony Windross: *All of the Balls and None of the Bollocks*   20
Helena Woddis: *The Stuff of Dreams*   29
Magus Minor: *Follow the Star*   37
Penny Mawdsley: *A Busy Decade*   41
John Theodore Cragg: *Still Hankering*   47
Peter Bellenes: *The Scent of the Roses*   50
Trevor Greenfield: *Will You Still Love Me Tomorrow?*   52
Bobbie Stephens Wright: *A Sense of Self*   56
Ken Smith: *Now, Here*   63
Richard Hall: *I Was in the Fabled Black Book*   67
Joanna Clark: *Kindness is the Greatest Virtue*   75

POETRY
Anne Ashworth: *Variations on a Given Theme*   79
Kathleen McPhilemy: *The Elephant in the Garden*   81
Sebastian Barker: *Scarlet Rose*   82
Hilary Davies: *Scarlet Rose*   83
William Oxley: *Interlocking Worlds*   84
Lynne Wycherley: *The Substitute Sky*   85
Sylvia Moody: *Harm Done*   86
Christopher Truman: *Eden Water*   87
Mimi Khalvati: *The Streets of La Roue*   88
John of the Cross: *The End of the Canticle*   94
Sebastian Barker: *The Walking Heart*   95

Adele Davide: *Oldies Abroad in Spring* 96
Dinah Livingstone: *Maytime* 97
Daphne Rock: *Peter Bellinger Brodie* 98
Tom Rubens: *At the Grave of Herbert Spencer* 99
Anne Beresford: *End of Book* 101

PROSE
Dominic Kirkham: *A Chronicle of the Ages
            of Life on a Small Planet* 102
Helen Bellamy: *This Life in the Physical World* 110
Anna Sutcliffe: *My Life and Colourful Times* 119
Alison McRobb: *Real Teachers Want to Explore* 122
Wendy Funnell: *St Matthew's Life of Jesus* 130
John Challenor: *In Praise of SOF's Stated Purpose* 136
David Paterson: *Atheist Priest* 138
Denis Gildea: *Political Morality* 146
Victor Anderson: *Ecology and the Strangeness of the Present* 150

NOTES ON CONTRIBUTORS 159

ACKNOWLEDGMENTS 164

NOTE ON SOF NETWORK 165

AFTERWORD BY JOHN BUNYAN 166

INDEX OF AUTHORS 169

Introduction

This Life on Earth has thirty-eight contributors, nineteen women and nineteen men, twenty-three prose pieces and fifteen poets. The prose pieces are all by members or associates of the SOF Network, which takes its name from the television series *Sea of Faith*, made by Don Cupitt in 1984, about the retreat of supernatural religion. Don Cupitt, of course, took the title of his TV series from Matthew Arnold's poem 'Dover Beach':

> The Sea of Faith
> Was once, too, at the full, and round Earth's shore
> Lay like the folds of a bright girdle furled.
> But now I only hear
> Its melancholy, long, withdrawing roar…

This intensely gloomy poem, said to have been written by Arnold on his honeymoon,[1] provided Don Cupitt's historical TV series with an excellent catchy title, which, however, has proved somewhat misleading as the name for the resulting Network. Perhaps that is why members now increasingly use the acronym SOF. The SOF Network does *not* deplore the decline in supernatural belief. It regards religion as a wholly human creation and a vital part of our human cultural treasury. It explores and sifts religious stories and teachings, trying to keep the gold and discard the harmful dross. The touchstone is *humanity*.

This Life on Earth has a wider remit than its predecessor *This is My Story*, edited by Teresa Wallace and published in 1998, which did very well and has now sold out. The brief in the *Call for Submissions* for the new title was *This Life on Earth*, either as 'my life, my personal story' or 'my thoughts about this life on Earth in

---

1 The last two lines of the poem are: 'Swept with confused alarms of struggle flight,/Where ignorant armies clash by night.' One can't help wondering whether things weren't going too well!

general' or both. I was delighted by the lively and varied response to my *Call for Submissions* and was forced to make a selection from the many pieces sent in, ending up with twenty-three articles. I should like to thank all those who submitted, whether I was able to include their work or not.

This Life on Earth begins with a short personal account by Don Cupitt, continues with a rich assortment of more life stories or quests, followed by essays on the state of our beautiful, now intensely vulnerable planet, and accounts from scientists, artists, teachers, civil servants, political writers and others.

What is this life on Earth without poetry? As most of the submissions from SOF members were in prose (though some did send in poems which are in the book), I cast my net wider and asked for contributions from poets beyond the Network. They came pouring in. Some of the best and some of the worst poetry in English has been on 'religious' or 'life' themes and when I became editor of *Sofia* I promised myself I would only publish poems I liked. For this book I had plenty to choose from and I am very grateful indeed to all the poets who sent in work, although space permitted me to publish only a small selection. All the poets chosen are contemporary, except for one sixteenth-century Spanish mystic, who lives on in his poetry.

One of the delightful aspects about editing *Sofia* is that whenever I have contacted people, even complete strangers, however distinguished or eminent, asking them to write something or for permission to reprint something in the magazine (for no pay!), they always say yes. Likewise, I have been delighted by the response from the poets whom I invited to submit poems for the book.

*

From time to time people ask: What is SOF Network? It seems rather amorphous. From time to time people make strenuous efforts to whip it into shape and don't get very far. SOF is not an army or a corporation but, more 'sof'ly', being a network enables it to produce a magazine, *Sofia,* run conferences and engender many other meetings. Thinking about this, I was rather reminded of the Demogorgon in Shelley's *Prometheus Unbound.* The Demogorgon was 'shapeless; neither limb nor form, nor outline; yet we feel it is a living Spirit.' Or perhaps it would be better to see the Network as *part* of that Demogorgon, spreading both inside and outside the churches. In the story, Prometheus is bound to a rock by the vengeful tyrant Jupiter for stealing fire from heaven to give to human beings, and also giving them language. It is the Demogorgon who arrives in the 'Car of the Hour', unseats Jupiter – the supernatural Almighty Ruler, 'the Nobodaddy Aloft' – and casts him down into the abyss, following which Prometheus is released.

On the other hand, Shelley's mother-in-law Mary Wollstonecraft, author of *The Rights of Women,* wrote to her lover Gilbert Imlay, whom she met in Paris at the time of the French Revolution: 'Imagination is the true fire stolen from heaven to animate this cold creature of clay, producing all those fine sympathies that lead to rapture, *rendering men social by expanding their hearts.'* All supernatural stories, including the story of Prometheus, are poetic tales produced by the human imagination and as such, a great common treasury. 179 years after the French Revolution, in May 1968, students echoed Wollstonecraft with their slogan on the walls of the Sorbonne: *'L'imagination au pouvoir!:* Power to the imagination!'. This year 2009 we celebrated Mary Wollstonecraft's 250th birthday in Old St Pancras Church in London, where she married William Godwin and has her tombstone. Her words were read out in the church.

Abelard, the renowned twelfth-century teacher in the Paris schools, wrote a book called *Sic et Non:* 'Yes and No'. Perhaps that describes SOF's attitude to religion: No to tyranny and all the abuse committed in the name of a supernatural Sanctioner. Yes to the treasures of wisdom and knowledge accumulated in the world's religions. Certainly a bleak rationalism is a very etiolated form of humanity. We need all our bodily, scientific, philosophical, imaginative and poetic powers, both to become as fully developed human individuals as possible during our brief span of life on Earth, and to confront the problems facing humanity as a whole.

This Life on Earth is many curious and particular autobiographies, together with a powerful admixture of poems and essays – a warning and a celebration. I hope it will bring pleasure to readers and food for thought.

Dinah Livingstone
London, May 2009

Changes and Chances

Don Cupitt

The saga of Joseph and his brothers in *Genesis* is a lengthy romantic fiction, extending over some 14 chapters. But it is more than just a secular folktale, because the whole narrative is shot through with a vivid sense of Divine Providence guiding the course of events so as to preserve Israel and his sons. At the end of the whole story Joseph looks back to the time, decades earlier, when his jealous brothers had beaten him, stripped him and sold him into slavery. 'You meant evil against me; but God meant it for good, to bring it about that many people should be kept alive, as they are today' (*Genesis* 50:20).

This idea of an overruling Providence or 'hidden hand' that quietly guides events and brings good out of evil has been immensely influential. In its strongest form it is the doctrine of the divine predestination of the whole history of the created world. No event whatever is merely accidental. Everything is *meant* to happen as it does. If you really believe this, you will not gamble, and you will hold no insurance policies. Nor will you tolerate any form of euthanasia, because God has already scheduled the manner and the moment of your death. But if you have ever really experienced divine Grace, you will feel utterly 'assured' of your own final 'perseverance' unto salvation (as the puritans used to put it). This is a very blissful kind of knowledge, and indeed, so attractive is the idea of a corrective hidden hand at work behind the superficially-contingent course of things that secular forms of it survive to this day, in capitalist ideas about the wisdom of 'the market' and in James Lovelock's 'Gaia' hypothesis.

In my own 20s, and especially around the years 1955-63, I was a realistic theist and really did see my own life, and all events, as being 'meant' and guided in every detail. My life seemed to have a ready-made shape. I had no home of my own, no money to speak of, and felt very free and happy. I just let things happen, and awaited what God would send. I did not attempt to plan a 'career', and to this day I have never drawn up my own *curriculum vitae* in order to apply for a job. Instead of a planned career, I had only 'what God wanted me to do' to rely upon. This was enough: I felt sure that in the end I would be looked after, and the story of my life would make sense.

Then, gradually, over the next twenty-odd years everything changed. Instead of seeing my own life as a preordained gift handed to me in daily instalments, I began to see it as a chapter of accidents, and only one of a great number of other possible lives that I might have lived instead. I am now surrounded by a bunch of reproachful ghosts – all other possible selves I might have become but either rejected or somehow let slip, and all my lost loves.

Worse, I hardly know what sense to make of my own life, or what kind of story to tell about it. Since the meaning of my life is no longer laid on for me, I have to make it for myself. But how? I was once asked to try to write an autobiography, and duly made the attempt, but it was a complete failure. In general, I have found that I cannot write to a market, or to order. My self seems to be rather loose-knit and unsettled. I've got an obstinate, hopeless devotion to freedom, and am only any good when I'm doing my own unpredictable thing. And what is my own thing? – it's what analytical philosophy would call 'thoroughgoing subjectivism'. Others might call it 'postmodernism'. At any rate, it has led me to back a bunch of losers: the poor old Church of England, academic theology, and the writing of too many books that always infuriate many more people than they please. Certainly they destroyed my 'career' – if that matters. And yet, and yet, in spite of everything, I do still feel able to say Amen to my own life. I'm so obstinate that I wouldn't change any of it, and I refuse to disown anything that I have done. There have been mistakes, of course, as well as all the accidents, and bad periods, too; but even though it's all been such a jumble and I am now surrounded by the ghosts of so many lost loves, impossible loves and might-have-beens, I still do not wish to change anything. Let it be.

Has there been any single thread running through it all? From adolescence I knew that I was of a speculative and religious disposition, and that somehow the pursuit of a spiritual good would be my chief concern. Just *what* good, and how to describe it, I did not know at first. Was it God, the supreme good, the good life, or the Truth? Or was I just trying to write a book that would really satisfy me: trying to reach and to articulate a vision of things in which I could at last find peace of mind? I'm not sure: when you are on a *quest*, as distinct from a pilgrimage, your conception of what it is that you are looking for gradually changes as you go along. Why, and how, you probably don't know. But you do feel pretty sure that if you ever find it, you will know it at once.

As one gets older, one tends to become more grumpy and impatient, and very reluctant to believe that one has anything to learn from anyone younger than oneself. To avoid disappearing up a cul-de-sac in that way, getting more lonely and extremist, I have tried (especially in the past decade or so) to turn my thinking and writing more towards ordinary people, ordinary language, and ordinary life. That has been a help – and indeed we all of us have to strike a balance between the self and society; between the pursuit of a purely personal project in life and the pursuit with others of common, social objectives.

Recently, after sixty years, I have however finally ceased to be an active (that is, a communicant) member of my own Church, the Church of England. It has not been easy, after so long, and I feel a wrench every Sunday morning; but I felt I had to make the symbolic gesture, because as things stand the Church will apparently go to almost any lengths to keep fundamentalists within the fold, but it will not do anything to retain the allegiance of modern, doubting people. It will not fully reconcile itself to, and commit itself to, the restless, modern, 'critical' style of thinking. To my mind, the Church's kind of religion is historically obsolete and doesn't work any more. I feel that I've got to move on, and try to make something new that will work better. I know I probably will not succeed, but perhaps I may be the writing on the wall – an indication that we do urgently need religious change and renewal.

There is not much time. For some decades now writers have been troubled by apocalyptic visions of a huge catastrophe threatening humanity. It now seems much more likely than not that we will get 4°C climate change and large areas of the Earth becoming uninhabitable well within the lifetime of the youngest people now alive. After that, there will be worse. I'm beginning to think more and more about how we are to prepare ourselves for and to cope with the reduction of the human race to a very small fraction of their present numbers, and living under very unfavourable conditions. What legacy do we want to leave to these people, our descendants? After the end of our present type of industrial civilisation it may take a thousand years or so for the Earth to cool down and get into balance again. What values, what intellectual methods and what ideas will our descendants be seeking to preserve during their long wait for better times?

No Safe Comforts

John Pearson

I first wrote this piece, or one essentially the same, some eleven years ago. Has nothing changed you may ask? Nothing much, except the timing and a few of my circumstances. For nothing has happened which has made my beliefs (or lack of) any different. This is a mark either of stubbornness or constancy. I prefer to see it as the latter. The greatest difference: my wife has been ordained as an MSE (Minister in Secular Employment in the Church of England, still employed full time in her University post). Have I softened my Atheist tendencies? No, indeed I have hardened them. So, to my story:

For over 30 years I have harboured suspicions that God is *not* in fact in his heaven and that maybe all is *not* well with the world. I'm sure that many, whether members of SOF Network or not, must feel something similar? Increasingly, I feel decisively that my own personal exploration of religion has shown me that it is just, and only, a human creation. So, perhaps I should declare my exploration ended, and resign from the Network? Maybe it has been, as someone once said, a 'demob camp' for those on the way out of the Church, and that I am well and truly 'out'. Colleagues at work are amazed that I devote two whole days of my annual leave to a conference designed to discuss something which doesn't exist. They have better things to do, they say, and shouldn't I?

I have only my own experiences from which to build the collage which you will view. They may seem naive perhaps, rather basic, but have been very real in shaping me. These awakenings, as I have called them, have merged to build the walls within which I dream my daydreams, the only defence I have against my fears. They start from an early age and together illuminate my move from a contentment born of a simple, loving and very sheltered Christian home since my adoption at 18 months of age, through to the 'nihilistic atheism', in which some have suggested I live today.

To begin, I fly back through time some 45 or 50 years to the cosy world of a quiet village in Warwickshire, the Squire in his big house (long since turned into a housing estate), and garden parties in the grounds of the home of some ex-colonial Governor. It might still have been 1914: Sunday School at the back of church, where the more imaginative or morbid of us cast weekly sidelong glances at an old lead pipe in which, a caption declared, a human head was found (was it there still? would it come out to haunt us?); 'winning' stickers for one's attendance; the crackers at the church Christmas party; standing beside my father as he confidently sang the harmony to all the hymns, or chanted plainsong from his old faded blue psalter; sitting sucking boiled sweets beside him as he sagely listened to interminable sermons; walking home beside him to roast beef and Yorkshire pudding, at a slight trot to keep up with his long be-suited strides. All so conservative, all so safe; no questioning, no doubt. As a child of eight I was taken to Christmas Morning service in nearby Rugby School chapel, with its powerful memorial window to Old Boys lost in the Great War (Rupert Brooke amongst them). I knew one had to be good here, to earn access to all the presents around the tree back home – the Protestant 'be-good-now-and-you'll-deserve-your-presents-later' ethic. In time I would move on, first to prep school and then to public school in York, with its chapel, its chaplain and its wise old masters, all selling a certain life-set – little questioning, little doubt. In those days, God *was* in his heaven and all *was* well with the world.

Alongside all this there was so much of which I was not aware, or to which I was not really exposed. Perhaps as the only child of fairly elderly parents I was inevitably sheltered from much outside. I was oblivious to all those who were *not* in our little village church, those who didn't come to the Garden Party or the church Christmas Party.

One detail which I did notice has remained with me ever since I was six or less, and could have shown me, even then, that there was something different about the way the 'other half' lived. One particular Sunday my father had to call on some church business at one of the small cottages opposite the church. An elderly couple came to the door together, and from behind them there was nothing: no familiar sound of *The World This Weekend* from the wireless and, above all, no familiar smell of roast beef, or pork, or lamb, or of the leathery dark green cabbage, which I loved. In short, no Sunday Dinner! During my walk (trot) back to my secure world I asked my father why they had no Sunday Dinner. I don't remember exactly what he said, but it was something to the effect that not everybody was as lucky as us – not that different people lived different lifestyles, but that not everybody was as lucky. Perhaps this brief exchange sowed the seeds of a social conscience – of an awareness in me of others – which still needs a little help, even today.

I struggled through my first few years of 'big school' with few friends, in a blind faith-driven world of my own, instilled in me from home: love thy neighbour; do unto others as you would be done to yourself (more *Water Babies* than Bible, but all part of the collage); if a man strikes you offer him the other cheek; if he asks for your coat give him your shirt too. My parents were mild people, who expected the world always to treat you *fairly*. Their son, in consequence, allowed his life to be made a bit of a misery for a number of years. My father loved me, and was not afraid to complain if he thought I was being bullied, but he would never encourage retaliation. So sometimes the bullying continued, or worsened, and the 'other cheek' became increasingly sore. (An alternative bit of scripture such as 'an eye for an eye' was presumably missing from father's book). I took comfort in the hope that my tormentors would meet their just deserts at the Day of Judgement. I just wished it would come soon. I remember feeling an immense relief, rejoicing even, when one particularly nasty bully was killed in a car crash one school holiday. In a rather un-Christian way, I suppose, I could have jumped for joy. I used to argue with my godless peers that, for me, God did exist. He most certainly did in those days, would see me alright, they'd see. ('Hadn't he rid me of the nasty bully?' I thought.)

I was rather hurt, I suppose, whilst secretly admiring his self-assurance (or freedom?) when my best friend chose, actually 'chose' he said, not to be confirmed. For me, life so far had all led irrevocably to this religious milestone. Confirmation was a rite of passage, so automatic that I of course failed to question it. Dutifully I both learnt and believed all the words, for my own sake as much as for Mum and Dad's.

Simultaneously, somewhere inside I had always had a shy admiration for the irreverent. I marvelled at stage-hands at public events, carrying on with their work rather than standing to attention for the National Anthem; contractor's men working to repair the foundations of York Minster whilst services carried on all around. Wouldn't they all be struck down in some way? At home, Dad railed against the new world – the Beatles and the like. Part of me couldn't wait to rebel. Now I am 'grown up' it is too late. Everybody is irreverent now, so there is less satisfaction to be gained from it. At church I do shocking things like missing out bits of the Creed, only to find that others do likewise. I once refused communion altogether when a stand-in priest didn't do things 'our way', but others joined me. Is the SOF Network just a clever way to rebel, a safe, middle-class atheism?

At 16, a young 16, I still believed in a God who could intervene and work miracles. So, I earnestly prayed for the safe return of the Apollo 13 astronauts, my greatest heroes at the time. Only as I came to my A-Levels did I finally develop real terminal doubt. I remember one particular event as clearly as I remember that missing Sunday Dinner. In chapel, at school, the sixth form were never unduly reverent. During our final weeks the chaplain once asked God's help for those taking their examinations. Near me, David (not his real name, as they say) was perfunctory. 'Sod him, I'll pass anyway.' This hurt. How could he be so complacent? ('Hope he fails for that,' I thought). As you might guess, David passed his Oxbridge entrance exam. All my life thus far I had lived with the saying that 'God looks after his own', albeit confused by its neighbour: 'God helps those who help themselves' – the latter a convenient, cruel exclusion clause thrown at those who fail, having trusted too much in the former. Later, our economics master suggested, regarding our A-Levels, that we take the advice given by Wellington on the eve of Waterloo which he paraphrased thus: 'Tonight you may pray like mad; tomorrow you must fight like hell'.

Ever since facing my first undergraduate exam I have never again put my faith in a God who might, or might not, intervene on my behalf. Rather, I have tried to work as hard as I could, as this seemed a more effective insurance policy. I have often passed since. So *what* God?

Other things have struck me besides the missing Sunday Dinner, the exam and the like. I married in good faith, quite literally at the time, within the reassuring mantle of 'those whom God hath joined together, let no man [or wicked woman?] put asunder'. It was a revelation to me, a sharp attack on my innocence, to learn during Family Law lectures, a few years later, that marriage was a legal estate, not a spiritual one. Like a contract it could be ended just as easily as it could be established, providing certain procedures were observed. I knew of course that couples could get a divorce, but it was as if a blind had suddenly shot up, illuminating yet another crack in the foundations. Hopefully, a couple may wish to spend the rest of their lives together in a contented way, but they may not. So *what* God?

Over the years I have read very many books on the Great War, from novels to collections of memoirs – certainly the most powerful influence throughout my life (memories of Rugby Chapel). I have always had a strong, perhaps perverse, urge to share the horrific camaraderie of the troops, living and dying in their tens of thousands. The more I read the more it seems totally inconceivable that an otherwise 'loving, caring' God, as they say, could allow such loss. So much needless suffering of so many – 'those who die as cattle'. The following piece poignantly offsets the harsh reality of which I have spoken against the innocent faith of a child. The Rev. Julian Bickersteth, senior chaplain to the 56th (London) Division, spoke to certain men on the eve of the first day of the battle of the Somme. He writes:

> I joined Major Lindsay, who has been so much help to me in my Church of England work with the London Scottish. He spoke to me of his wife and child and told me of the joy he had in his little boy's faith and the wonder of his childish prayers, and went on to say how confident he felt that he would come through safely. 'The faith of my little boy is so real. He prays every night for my safety. God could not disappoint a faith like that.' I never saw him again. He was shot dead in the advance the next morning.

So, *what* God ?

Two years ago I made my first visit to the Somme. As a medal collector I was keen to visit the actual sites of the actions, to see for myself the graves of those who had died so far from home, to pay some personal homage. I went there quite open to any feelings which they might stir. What I did feel, in fact, particularly in one small cemetery, the evening sun seeping softly through the trees as I read the names of men and boys, was a tremendous sense of calm. I wrote on my return of how much I envied them. I longed for a little cared-for plot of my own – 'some corner of a foreign field that is for ever England'.

Wars affect me, major famine affects me, a close friend's autistic son for whom there appears to be no cure affects me. Once I might have expected God to have helped out. But we seem to have either a powerless God (useless) or a powerful God who doesn't attend to the right problems (worse than useless). Maybe we should judge God as we might a politician? How does he or she cope with the big problems? So, *what* God?

Since my visit to France both my own parents have died: my mother, the dutiful attentive wife of the 'old school' and my father, schoolteacher and pillar of the community. And what do I feel? Are they in Heaven? They lie in peace (at peace?) in a quiet corner of an English churchyard. They are still down there, I trust, bodies gently wearing away. What lives on? Personally, I feel that people are still alive 'in spirit' as long as there are others who remember them in person, in whose minds they live on. I once saw a TV play in which an elderly widower would sit in his garden, asking himself how his wife would have responded to each of his problems. It was as if she were still alive. She did not live on in any natural (or supernatural) way, but her presence was as powerful as ever, as long as he could summon her to mind. Don Cupitt talks in his writings of visiting and even talking to graves, and how this can have a certain power. My parents are now long gone and I visit their graves very rarely but sometimes I do still ask myself how they might have handled my problems. Perhaps, through this, they have begun to live for ever.

As I write this, I am secretary of St Thomas's Church here in Newcastle. Is this not an inappropriate post for a self-confessed atheist, nihilist even? My wife, not surprisingly, has some reservations on this score. I myself see it as my repayment to a system which has served me well. Arriving in Newcastle, I found true friends, and my wife-to-be; more a tribute to their Christianity than mine, I suppose. I saw people doing genuinely good work for the poor and homeless of the city, all those latter-day Sunday-lunchless poor old souls. St Thomas's was doing much that the congregations of many other churches appeared too proud to do. It was, in those far off days, the spur for much local social challenge; a forum for many ideas that still lacked real mainstream acceptance. We hosted some of the region's first exhibitions in support of Gay rights, on the plight of the homeless, and against Apartheid.

St Thomas's still awaits the major re-fit I hoped for eleven years ago, to equip it to return to its former role of active caring.

It will be staffed mostly by people who see themselves as doing God's work. Maybe they are, if there is a God. For me it will simply be fulfilling its natural role in the community of which, geographically, it is at the centre. For as long as it needs a secretary, and others – not wanting the job themselves – are happy for me to continue, then I shall oblige. I offer energy and interest, I can offer no more.

Despite the doubts which I expressed in my opening remarks, I think I shall indeed stay on in the Network, just as I have stayed on at St Thomas's. I get an awful lot out of it, not least the companionship of good friends of broadly like mind. Perhaps because I think there is a job to be done, enabling others to get support in their own search for a special kind of happiness and freedom. Or maybe I just feel the need of people who can help me continue to grow, to face the harsh world in which I have to get along, to help me make the most of my remaining 40 years or so. For in reality I have no quiet corner of a foreign field, and somebody or something must help me take my leave, one day, without the safe comfort of the promise of a Heaven.

It Belongs to Us All

Cicely Herbert

The older I become, the more haunted I am by the opening lines of T.S.Eliot's *Four Quartets* and I become ever more certain that time cannot be a simple linear progress from point A, and on into infinity:

> Time present and time past
> Are both perhaps present in time future,
> And time future contained in time past.

Whenever I visit my favourite building in London, the Covent Garden Opera House, I am struck by the way this beautifully restored theatre is inhabited by the ghosts, or the spirits, from its past. I have known the building ever since, as a twenty year old, I got a job there as an usherette, and was paid to receive what became my musical education. Many years later, I took a group of 'ex-offenders', all women, to look around the newly restored opera house. I assured them that the building belongs to us all, and that it contains the best facilities in London, which they are as entitled as anyone else to use. Outside, where until recently the fruit and vegetable market had spilled over the roads and pavements, we watched the street performers, buskers, singers, and fire-eaters, entertaining passers-by, as they have done, in that area, for centuries. London, with its well-defined 'villages' is ever adapting to the times, and yet its spirit remains constant, as it greets and shelters refugees and runaways, entrepreneurs and bankers, conmen and saints.

It is perhaps in the more remote areas, where time seems to have stood still for centuries, that one becomes aware of the anachronisms of modern life. As jet planes fly perilously low over ancient moorlands, tearing the sky apart, life in the small hamlets and villages is catching up with the technology of the twenty-first century. It was in a remote village of 600 inhabitants that I saw, outside its single shop, a sign advertising their 'INTERNET CAFÉ: Access to the Whole World'.

In January 2000, at my brother's funeral in Northumberland, I met a woman who confessed to me that she couldn't help feeling happy, because she had, that very day, become engaged. When I asked where her fiancé was, she told me that he lived in Hungary and she had yet to meet him. Her romance had been conducted over the internet. What seemed then an extraordinary way to conduct affairs of the heart, may not seem so strange in the future.

I have a good life, and I cannot imagine wanting anything more from it than I have now. However, my childhood, at least from the day that my mother was diagnosed with TB, was pretty miserable. It is only now, more than 60 years later, that I am able to consider what my mother's illness must have meant to my parents. Each had lost a brother in active service over the two world wars. In 1945, when my father was demobbed from the Air Force, my parents were reunited and prepared to return to their former lives. We left London and went home to the North. The brass plate on our front gate was polished up and former patients were advised that my father was available to act again as their family doctor.

However, when my chain-smoking mother conceived and gave birth to her third child, my sister, it became clear that she was very unwell. She was diagnosed with TB, and sent to a sanatorium in Switzerland, where she remained for a long time. My seven-year-old brother and I were dispatched to boarding schools and I learned to identify my mother with postcards showing picturesque, clean little children, edelweiss, cowbells, and snow-capped mountains, and she grew unreal to me, almost like a dream, a figment of my imagination.

During the school holidays we three children were sent off to live with various kindly Scottish aunts and uncles and occasionally, with long-suffering patients of my father's. For many years we barely visited our home. It was when I was fourteen, and staying with a school friend in Yorkshire, where I was as unhappy as I have ever been, that I became aware that, while my hosts lived in a mansion, surrounded by a tranquil, flower-filled garden and green fields, nearby was another, grimy world of poverty and deprivation. The house stood between the two industrial cities of Rotherham and Sheffield, and the distant smoke from the steel works was clearly visible from their tennis court. I felt out of place in the heart of a family that was so at ease with itself and its position in life, and my feeling of alienation increased daily. I must have been an ungrateful guest, who preferred to stand out in the hall, and read a book, rather than join in the family's games and conversation. It soon became apparent that my behaviour was considered unacceptable. When we went back to school the next term, I had become an outcast, as, one by one, my group of friends turned away from me. Unhappy as I was, from that moment, I set myself firmly on the side of those who endured hardship and poverty, and it is only in recent years that I have gained a more balanced view of the realities of life.

Such teaching as I have done, has been with disadvantaged adult learners, many of whom had real talents and gifts that had never been nurtured or recognised. This particularly applied to most of the ex-offenders I have been privileged to work with, gifted women, some of whom were exceptionally bright, whose lives, for one reason or another, had gone badly amiss, and who faced an uphill struggle to re-enter mainstream life after imprisonment or probation. As things are today, far too many people leave school feeling that they have been thrown on the scrap heap before their lives have begun to take off. I believe that this life on Earth is the only one there is: we must give every person alive the chance to enjoy a share of its many riches.

All of the Balls and None of the Bollocks

Tony Windross

Sound bites are sometimes handy, but the publisher was having none of it. We were trying to find a suitable title for a book I'd nearly finished, one of the few written from an openly 'sofish' perspective. But he felt that however eye-catching it was, such a title (shown above) wasn't appropriate – not least because the *Church Times* would never review it! Something a lot safer was eventually chosen, and the book sold in encouraging numbers.[2] But I still think that such a title would have more accurately described the motivation behind it, as well as being something of a health-warning for anyone stumbling inadvertently across it. All too often religious liberals/radicals seem to feel a need to apologise for being who they are, and what they can't believe – and I wanted to make it clear that not only did I *not* feel like that, but as far as I was concerned, a non-realist faith had everything that was necessary, but with none of the weird bits that were usually part of the religious package.

Having been installed in a church choir at the age of eight by my religiously non-churchgoing parents, I'd left by the age of about thirteen, and spent much of the next twenty years sniggering at the church and all who sailed in her. The whole religion-thing was just *so* silly, and clearly of appeal only to the seriously inadequate: anyone with half a brain could see that, and therefore wouldn't want to get anywhere near it. At Cambridge I was mercifully never troubled by the ridiculous evangelicals from the CICCU,[3] whilst at Birmingham as part of the PGCE[4] course I was introduced to philosophy through the writings of the fiercely

---

2   *The Thoughtful Guide to Faith* (O Books, Winchester 2004) reprinted 2005).
3   Cambridge University Inter-Collegiate Christian Union.
4   Postgraduate Certificate of Education.

anti-religious writer Daniel O'Connor. He was a large part of the reason why I became a Logical Positivist, albeit thirty years or so after pretty well everyone else had stopped. I began working as a teacher, but spent much of my limited spare time working for an external London degree in philosophy. That was how I came across the writings of the blessed Wittgenstein, and his representative on Earth, D.Z. Phillips. And it was why once a year at Madingley Hall, Cambridge, a group of us would gather for a study weekend specifically arranged for external London BA philosophy students. They were challenging and stimulating affairs, but it was a source of considerable puzzlement for me to learn that two of the most thoughtful (and formidably intelligent) of my fellow students were also actively involved in their local churches. How *could* they take stuff like that seriously? (as John McEnroe might have put it).

Into this turmoil came the *Sea of Faith* television series and book, with the tipping point being Don Cupitt's appearance in person at one of those Madingley weekends. It wasn't a case of everything falling neatly into place – but of all sorts of possibilities opening up. So much so that a couple of years later, at the time of the first SOF Conference, I was seriously thinking about the possibility of ordination. It would be some time before that happened, however, because my theological views were not ones that the church authorities had ever really come across before in a potential ordinand – hardly surprising, given that I still have yet to meet *any* member of the clergy who felt called to ordination as a direct result of SOF! My position was paradoxical, which was why I was unable to make sense of it to myself, let alone anyone else. But as a result of the support and encouragement of a number of people (a debt I can never repay) I was eventually ordained. I worked for four years as a non-stipendiary minister, whilst keeping my day job of teaching; and then went into full-time parish ministry, where I've been for the last twelve years, first in Sussex, then Norfolk, and now Kent.

Given my radical perspective, and given that the ranks of the clergy are stuffed full with people exuding all sorts of certainties I've never had (or wanted), I've always felt something of an outsider. Although this can make for isolation, it does act as a constant reminder of the way that most thoughtful people *are* outsiders when it comes to religion. Most of them are unable to tick many (or maybe even any?) of the belief boxes, and feel disenfranchised from the church as a result. The fact that I'm able not just to survive in it, but also to engage fully with it, shows that faith and belief are very different things; that the Church of England at its best is a broad and generously inclusive church; and that even ultra-sceptics are (sometimes) welcome. But before that can become a possibility, the sceptics at the gates must be brought into contact with a way of looking at religion which can't simply be dismissed as mindless. The New Atheists of Dawkins, Hitchens and Co focus on the Fundamentalists because it's a bit like shooting fish in a barrel. Sofists and the like present much more of a challenge, which is why we often attract particular hostility from militant secularists. Their preconceptions and simplifications need to be confronted, and much of my energy for many years has been directed at trying to draw attention to the thoughtful and radical perspectives that exist.

I first got the idea at one of the SOFIC[5] gatherings in Loughborough, arranged for many years by the indefatigable Ronald Pearse, to whom many of us are hugely indebted. What was wanted, we were told, was a series of leaflets to publicise SOF, and some hastily-produced specimens were handed round for our inspection. As soon as I saw them it occurred to me that something in that format, with the specific intention of getting people to think about religious questions, could be put out at the back of my church in Norfolk – if only they existed. I went away determined to write something: within a couple of weeks I'd roughed-out three, and within a month I had six. They were short, provocative, and printed in eye-catching colours (one of

---

5   Sea of Faith in the Churches.

my wife's many splendid ideas). They each began with a question: Why Bother to Think about …God? the Bible? Prayer? and so on. The idea was to grab the casual visitor's attention as they wandered around the church, and to show that different perspectives really *were* possible, despite all the evidence to the contrary.

I put them out on display, having no idea how they would be received. In the event, not only was there no explosion of indignation, but instead a great deal of support – although the resulting publicity did eventually result in an invitation to explain my position to the area bishop. The amount of positive feedback meant that after a couple of years I began to wonder whether they could form the basis for a book, which would reach a much larger number of people. Despite the lack of enthusiasm already mentioned about the title, John Hunt encouraged me, and even agreed to publish the result. Mindful of what had happened to the shamefully-treated Anthony Freeman when he was in a similar position, it was with some trepidation that I showed the resulting manuscript to my diocesan bishop – but found him both positive and affirming. Reviews of the book were generally favourable, and invitations to speak to groups all over the country began to arrive. It was a busy time, but showed the hunger that existed for an approach to faith which did *not* involve trying to believe the unbelievable, and which might therefore be a real possibility for many of the people who were unreachable by means of the orthodox ways of thinking and speaking.

The world of religion really *is* another country: they do (and think) differently there. So differently, in fact, that to the thoughtful but uninitiated, it seems a bizarre and barmy place. My claim is that the profound spiritual riches to be found there are fully available to those who can do little or nothing with the concept of supernaturalism, and who find the idea of non-realism truly liberating. Such a slimmed-down, non-metaphysical faith really *does* have everything necessary for a healthy and vigorous spiritual life, but with none of the indigestible elements that make so many people gag. It's got all the life and energy of its doctrinally-bloated cousins, without the need for any of the mental gymnastics that go along with them. Given the way that fundamentalism and various forms of evangelicalism have come to dominate the airwaves in recent years, the sentiments that lay behind the original title of the book seem even more necessary if people on the outside are to be reached.

There *is* just so much bollocks talked in the name of religion! Those outside hear it and conclude that their lowest estimations are fully realised, which means they have more than enough reason to leave religion well alone. Those inside either swallow it all – or keep their heads down and mouths shut, whilst feeling guilty that they can't jump through the hoops they think they ought to be able to do. Hardly any of those inside call the purveyors of the bollocks to account, by demanding that the things said in the name of religion be subject to the sort of careful and thoughtful scrutiny that is expected in every other area of life.

Those who live by critical thinking *and* by faith simply can't allow things to go on like this any longer. To say and do nothing will mean that the church continues along its rapid downhill path as numbers diminish, with an ever-increasing proportion of those who remain occupying theological positions not far removed from certifiable lunacy. The problem is that most theological radicals have given up on the church, seeing it as beyond hope and incapable of reform. They've walked away, and pursue their journeyings in other ways. Almost the only views that are heard, therefore, from within the church are of the conservatives, whose very success sounds the death-knell of a thoughtful and self-critical faith.

But maybe the conservatives and the radicals are both right? Maybe it *is* impossible to sustain a non-realist position within the church; maybe those who think in such shocking ways need to get out and leave the church to the mindless? Maybe those of us inside may wake up tomorrow and decide that our position really *is* unsustainable, and that there's no alternative to throwing in our lot with the strident secularists. It's possible, of course – but it would be a desperate outcome for those of us who value beyond measure the spiritual and liturgical framework that the church provides, within which we can respond to the depths and mysteries of human existence. Honesty is usually the best policy, and it's surely time for far more of it in religion. The conservatives miss no opportunity to criticise those of a more thoughtful perspective, and we need to respond in kind. We need to refuse to have anything to do with the sexist and homophobic rantings of the extreme evangelicals; and we need to stand up for those whose voices are being silenced. We need also to refuse to have anything to do with the anti-intellectualism of the fearful, who are terrified that if they accept the findings of science when they conflict (as they often, not surprisingly, do) with the ancient texts, the whole religious edifice will crumble. They need to get a life – and to grow up!

Having run discussion and study groups where the only ground rules are that no questions are off-limits, it's clear that many church members are glad of the opportunity of expressing their doubts. For far too long the church has made people feel ashamed if they're not able to sign up to the whole doctrinal package, no matter how peculiar its demands. It's time for honesty and openness: for owning the struggles of the spiritual life, and accepting the validity of the many paths to truth. Of course it's risky, not least for clergy who might shock and enrage their congregations by daring to treat them as adults. But the alternative is even worse: namely, continuing to live a lie, to pretend, to be inauthentic. If the only way that the religious show can be kept on the road is through dissembling, then it's probably time to bring it to an end. SOF and open and inclusive groups such as PCN,[6] TCPC,[7] Inclusive Church and others, have a major role to play in trying to keep the rumour of God alive in the 21st century world. They may run out of steam in the long run but

---

6 Progressive Christianity Network.
7 The Center for Progressive Christianity (USA).

that's hardly the point. Keynes once memorably observed that 'In the long run, we are all dead!' – but we don't live in the long term. We're where we are, and must use whatever spiritual resources are to hand if we're to make of ourselves all that we could be.

Many people may have no need of religion at all, and manage to live fulfilled and generous lives that are completely secular. But there are also those of us who find religion not just helpful but pivotal – and therefore need to equip ourselves to survive in what can be a pretty hostile church environment. Without the support provided by SOF, and more specifically without the intellectual framework provided by Don Cupitt, it's difficult to see how I could ever have taken religion seriously as an adult. In the years BC (Before Cupitt) religion seemed to require me to give up my mind. But in the years AD (After Don) that particular burden has been lifted, and all questions are now permitted, and all-comers are welcome. Only in certain places, of course, but the existence of even the odd oasis means that survival is now possible (although not guaranteed).

The American philosopher of religion, Loyal Rue, began his remarks to the 1989 SOF Conference in the following way:

> The Church *is* precisely what the Church *says* it is, and the central proclamation of the Church is precisely what the Church *declares* it to be. [This means that] if all the intelligent, informed, and moral people were to leave the Church, then the Church would be left in the hands of those who are stupid, ignorant and wicked, in which case the central proclamation of the Church would be whatever stupidity, ignorance and wickedness declared it to be.

He went on:

> If intellectual rigour leaves the Church, then the Church will be left in the hands of stupid people. If tolerance leaves the Church, then the Church will be a haven for bigotry. If peace makers leave the Church then the Church will become an instrument of

war. If feminists leave the Church, then the Church will remain a source of unjust discrimination. And so on.

He spoke of the need for 'radical theological prophylactics, as a safeguard against the virus of conservative theology'. His message to the theologically dispossessed was 'for God's sake, don't leave the Church in the hands of the true believers ... What I'm trying to say is that to abandon the Church is not an acceptable option for those who are alienated by its failure to make its way beyond the 17th century. If the Church is left to the true believers there may one day *be* no refuge.'

That was 20 years ago – and the dangers are now even greater. Those years have seen an increasingly confident and frighteningly mindless anti-intellectualism take hold of the Church. Those inside who can't stomach such stuff have left in droves, whilst those outside who don't regard thinking as an optional extra have looked elsewhere for their spiritual sustenance. This is why there is a responsibility for those of us who love and value the Church to do all that we can to ensure that the fundamentalist-evangelical axis is not allowed to become the only show in town. War is often said to be too important to be left to the generals – and in similar vein, religion is too important to be left to the bishops, whose efforts to placate the numerically large conservatives are the kiss of death for anything radical. Those of us at the bottom of the food chain need to get involved, to stand up and be counted – and shot at. We need to show that not only do the evangelicals *not* have all the best tunes (with their choruses being about as profound as their theology) but that dignified and thoughtful religion is not an oxymoron. And although radical religious perspectives will never have anything other than a minority appeal, that in no way limits their significance; popular culture will always attract greater numbers than anything that demands genuine seriousness and the application of intelligence.

Few clergy speak out in favour of the sort of radical inclusiveness that is being argued for here. Perhaps because they don't believe in it? Perhaps because they are frightened for their jobs? Perhaps because they haven't dared to look the questions in the face? Who knows? But unless more are prepared to take whatever risks are involved, the future for any kind of organised religion that stands a chance of reaching the thinking, sceptical-by-nature classes is surely bleak. Without SOF and similar groups to keep things bubbling, it's surely impossible.

The Stuff of Dreams

Helena Woddis

... 'We are such stuff
as dreams are made on; and our little life
is rounded with a sleep.' – THE TEMPEST: IV:1

Three weeks ago I dreamt the unthinkable. In my dream, I quietly murdered a close friend in cold blood, in my garden, on the old wooden bench I can see now from my window. In the dream, it was an early spring day, cool sunshine, primroses under the cedar tree, a hopeful blackbird singing a nesting song, and who knows, perhaps the downstairs neighbours watching from their windows. Everything as real and close as it is today, waking.

I pottered around unselfconsciously in the dream, almost forgetful of what I had done. After a while, I thought that perhaps I should call someone to verify the death. The doctor perhaps, or an ambulance. What was the cause of death? Well, murder. Perhaps I should dispose of the evidence. Wouldn't that make life simpler for me? Clearly, I had no sense of anything wrongly done, merely than it might be inconvenient for me if it were known.

I began to search for the body, and for a long time couldn't find it. I had no feelings, no thoughts, except that it was a lovely day. When I finally did find the dead person, I was suddenly flooded with a sense of horror, disgust and fear – not at what I had done, but at what I must do. I must touch, penetrate and manipulate this cold, dead oozing corpse with my bare hands!

The horror was so great that I woke up. Four thirty. An hour and a half before sunrise. In the hours before dawn the body is at its lowest ebb, the imagination most vivid. I was alone, shocked, burdened with the unspeakable illogical meaning of what I had dreamt. I had never, waking, imagined killing anyone. But the most shocking thing was the sense of revulsion and horror I felt, and still felt, at touching the now dead body of someone I had, living, once loved.

What does this dream mean? Not much probably. I don't think there is much scientific knowledge to be gained from the literal interpretation of dreams, though Freud, in his desire to make psychoanalysis a science, wrote a whole book on it. Yes, perhaps I have wanted to murder someone at times. And I don't fancy touching the cold visceral insides of a dead person, least of all that of a friend. But what dreams chiefly tell us is not only what our deepest hopes and fears are, but what it means to be human in all its complexity. They shock us into a realisation of what we are, and we have to live with what we discover. In sleep, the moralistic big brother (and I had one of those in the real world!), who watches over and judges our behaviour, is dormant, and the vivid untrammelled unconsciousness, in all its wild secret life, can surface, bringing with it surprising images and thoughts devoid of all moral judgement. So dreams, even nightmares, are a kind of freedom; that part of us over which we have no mastery is free to range in the deep unvisited tunnels and underground rivers of the psyche, peopled by the monsters and witches and fairies which we are sometimes reluctant to own. We could become monsters, or we flee from monsters. Life can, as in my nightmare, be cheap, but death, at the same time, can be easy and a terrifying inevitable reality.

Weeks later, the shock of my dream is only just receding. I fell, that early pre-dawn, into a sickened sleep and dreamt some more common dreams; of being found, for example, in my nightclothes in the street by an early important visitor, and being unable to remember where I had put my day clothes. Familiar? That morning the day dawned painfully, and until I could find another person, just one, on whom to unburden myself, I just couldn't function. More than one would be unthinkable, because I was beginning to feel shame. How powerful are the emotions which take hold of us after a nightmare, even though we know we have done nothing in the cold light of day. Only the repeated conviction that I was actually innocent of my dream's events kept me from falling into misery. Eventually a good breakfast and an hour with my first client (I did find my clothes!) began to restore a sense of normality.

Carl Jung, the Swiss psychoanalyst, also, as a young man, dreamed the unspeakable. He saw God passing a great stool which fell onto the church below and shattered its roof. This was blasphemy to the young Carl; it was an image of God that had never before been allowed expression in his world. It shocked him (isn't it a fascinating thing that we can shock ourselves? It's as though the right hand doesn't always know what the left hand is doing). It shocked Jung to dream up such an image but also gave him a huge sense of relief. He had been brought up by a strictly religious Lutheran clergyman father, seven uncles who were pastors, and a mother steeped in folk superstition. No doubt any reference to bodily functions or sex were particularly scarce in Jung's home. So the dream, blasphemous as it was, meant a liberation, a freedom to think his own, even unthinkable, thoughts, and was the beginning of a great mind's autonomy.

What careful, decent people (like ourselves) do in dreams is often what we wouldn't dare do in reality. We do things which would shame, embarrass, frighten us – possibly liberate us too. But we all know somewhere deep down, that the things we dream are things we might be capable of, *in extremis*. The onset of senility, mental imbalance, fear, love, lust, or any strong passion, will allow the mysterious unconscious, the Id, to surface and drive out the injunctions of the moralistic Big Brother, Super-Ego, who is watching us. All hell can be let loose – and sometimes Heaven too.

It is no coincidence that the fathers of psychoanalysis chose Greek words to define the different chambers of the mind and the self. The ancient Greek myths, which like all myths are our myths too, match our dreams. The ancient Greek gods are not lofty, ethereal and virtuous beings. They are characters, not unlike the Old Testament God Yahweh, who come frequently down from Mount Olympus, and feel the human passions even more vividly than the humans themselves. They scrabble, are envious and competitive, they love and lust after beautiful youths and maidens, they manipulate and bargain and deceive both the mortals and each other, constantly displaying their superior power. 'As flies to wanton boys are we to the gods. They kill us for their sport.'[8]

The fascinating thing about ancient Greek drama is that it is the humans, and in particular the heroes, half god, half man, who have a profound and innate sense of natural justice. So we find them, with all their frailties and human desires, nonetheless pitted against the gods in their attempts to right injustice, to avenge unfair deaths, to restore rightful dynasties, and reunite feuding families. In addition to the passions, the Greek humans feel those emotions for which the gods have no time: loyalty, filial piety, doubt, remorse, grief and shame. Oedipus, for example, through no fault of his own, (he was 'unconscious' of his situation), breaks two powerful taboos – those of incest and patricide – and when he realises this, his shame and remorse are so great that he puts out his own eyes. Only in nightmare would we do such a thing, yet we understand the meaning of this act, and as we watch we are rent with pity and terror.

These myths become our own, because they are about us. They can express things which we experience only in nightmare, but fear in our waking life. A moment of unbalance, and we can imagine them happening to us. So it is with a strong sense of connecting with some essential truth that we watch these plays, as others have watched them for over two thousand years. Such art, though we might shudder, is a great delight and enrichment of our lives.

And because these myths belong to all of us, they didn't stop with the Greeks. The afternoon before my nightmare (and perhaps a contributor to it) I went to a performance of Arthur

---

8   *King Lear:* IV:1.

Miller's *A View from the Bridge*. I sat amongst a great swathe of GCSE-level students, all boys, on an afternoon out. I was with an ex-teacher, and our hearts sank slightly at the sight of these teenagers as the play began. But they behaved beautifully, because like ourselves, they were all gripped by the play and forgot to goof about. For them too, young though they were, this was the real thing, penetrating to the nub of human delight and pain, of uncontrollable passion but also natural justice. It was a splendid production and Miller held those boys' attention the whole way through. It was so strong an experience that even the usher asked afterwards, 'Did you enjoy it? It's amazing how it gets to you, isn't it?'

Miller had visited Syracuse, in Sicily, and stood in the wonderfully preserved Greek theatre there, and thought about how he could write about the same timeless themes with the same directness as the ancients. In *A View from the Bridge,* set in Brooklyn in the 1940s, the main protagonist, Ed brings up his orphaned niece, and realises, as she becomes 17, that he wants to protect her from the outside world, to keep her, in fact, for himself. Unconsciously, this is an incestuous urge, one which cannot be acknowledged, but which becomes clearer to Ed when it is threatened. A young relative of Ed's wife's, an illegal immigrant from Sicily, comes to live with them while he finds work. The young people become friends and eventually lovers, and Ed becomes so tormented by jealousy and his passionate desire for her that eventually he betrays the young man and his brother to the immigration authorities. Like Oedipus, he has broken taboos, but unlike Oedipus, he doesn't repent. He denies the real injustice of what he has done and gets into a fist fight with the young man's brother. Here again, Ed breaks the rules and draws a knife. Throughout the play, because of his passion, he defies natural justice; his punishment is his death in this fight, unrepentant, dishonoured, friendless, mourned, ironically, most of all by the niece he loved so much.

Dreams bring us into an altered state, because they are not reality. Theatre seems to excite and satisfy us because, in comedy as well as in tragedy, we are seeing something of life on this Earth, life which is reality in a heightened form. And so we are looking at ourselves, allowing ourselves to live vicariously experiences which we might not have the opportunity or the courage to live out personally.

Last week I experienced a different kind of dream, and a different drama, in the form of my only and much loved daughter's wedding in Hong Kong. (The nightmares hadn't stopped. I dreamt while there, just to keep the shadow in play perhaps, that my friendly old black Labrador Taylor had turned into the Hound of the Baskervilles, and was chewing off my right hand in a torrent of blood!) I had been troubled when Katharine told me last year that she was going back to work in advertising for a year to pay for the wedding she had always imagined. As a Quaker I was concerned that the testimony to simplicity was being thoroughly overlooked. I also dreaded the twelve-hour flight in steerage and a completely unknown city to be managed when Katharine was clearly going to be taken up with the 35 friends who were flying out to join her. So I went with anxiety, feeling too my utter inadequacy as the mother-of-the-bride, who had contributed nothing from the other side of the world.

But the experience altogether became an enchantment, handled with creative delicacy and elegance, with deep commitment to producing a golden experience for all the people Katharine loves, and a significant rite of passage for the young couple. The sun shone all day (it doesn't often do that in Hong Kong), the breeze from the sea was gentle, the guests all arrived from Hong Kong Island in an old junk, the timing was perfect. There were orchids in willow branches, little lanterns for after dark, tiny flower girls and Katharine in a lovely gown. Nothing was missing, nothing superfluous. This was a humanist wedding, the registrar a jolly smiling fellow in a linen jacket, and the couple had written their own vows. So harmonious, simple and sincere did it all seem to me that I was won over. I was not only won over, I was bowled over, deeply touched, horribly tearful (but I am the mother of the bride, so that was alright!) unspeakably proud. I think I experienced an altered state, and lost myself completely for that day and several days following.

This was theatre, a creation, but it was real, it was meaningful, it was about someone infinitely dear to me making a vow of fidelity to someone infinitely dear to her. They were climbing into a small boat together and facing the waves of uncharted waters. They were also doing the most normal and natural thing in the world: coupling. It didn't feel ordinary to me though. It felt huge and brilliant and wonderful, and it will stay with me, every minute of it, like a great Greek play or a modern drama, for years to come, as I keep on hoping that the vows will be fulfilled.

So what is this life on Earth? I have lived out my allotted time, all but one year, of three score years and ten. My life has been rich and varied. It has had passion and disappointment, love and loneliness, family closeness and family separations. There have been dramas and even tragedies, embarrassments and comedy, but the human spirit seems to be about enduring and learning, and although, like everyone else, I feel like a foolish kid at times, I think I am learning wisdom. I have learnt that life is not the pursuit of happiness. That way lies madness. Nor is it about achieving virtue or winning laurels. It is for me about an open-hearted acceptance of everything that is: pain, pleasure, flatness, excitement, fulfilment and failure, hope, tears and laughter. I think we are on this Earth to experience as fully as we can what comes to us, to tussle with it and make it our own, and revel in the opportunity. So my daughter's wedding brought me a fairytale lived in hope by real people: the theatre, which has always been just about my favourite place to be, brings me a mirror held up dramatically to real life: and what surfaces into semi-consciousness in the dead of night reminds me that I am human, not flawed, but certainly capable of evil as well as of good.

Perhaps this is Don Cupitt's *Solar Living,*[9] but with the addition of the night-time and of the moon.

I think I shall probably live another twenty-five years. What I hope most for is to preserve the faculties, not only of sight and hearing, but of imagination, so that all these dramas will remain as vivid for me in old age as they are to me now. And just think:

> To die, to sleep;
> To sleep: perchance to dream; ay, there's the rub;
> For in that sleep of death what dreams may come
> When we have shuffled off this mortal coil,
> Must give us pause.[10]

There could be nightmares even in the sleep of death, and if so, perhaps there could be sweet vivid fulfilling dreams too. But my guess is that, when all is over, we shall simply sleep, all passion spent.

---

9   Don Cupitt, *Solar Ethics* (SCM Press, London 1995).
10 *Hamlet:* III:1.

Follow the Star

Magus Minor

I am writing as a retired priest of the Church of England. I have been retired for many years and during this time my views have changed in an agnostic, and even atheistic direction. My impression is that this movement has taken place for a number of priests and bishops in recent years. I do not like the phrase 'loss of faith'. Life, and mental life, is a journey and if one moves closer to truth it is not loss but gain. To me the most important things in life are love and truth. All the time we are searching for truth. Needless to say there are numerous questions for which we shall never know the answers but the evidence is that human beings can progress towards truth. This development is shown very clearly in science where clearly we know much more about the true nature of the universe than was known in the past. Religion is not science but here too surely there has been progress.

Luckily while I was in the active ministry I was not troubled about the truth of Christian doctrine but since I retired I have had much more time to read and think and this has led to my change of view. The first influence has come from scholarly biblical criticism. This shows that the gospels are not accurate history in our sense of the word. They were written many years after the death of Jesus by believers. They felt it was perfectly fair to describe or even invent incidents in Jesus' life as though they were the fulfilment of Old Testament prophecy. St John's was written last and this is the gospel in which we get the clearest statements that Jesus was divine, phrases such as 'I and my Father are one'. Jesus spoke in Aramaic and the gospels are in Greek. It is unlikely that any of the long discourses in St John's gospel were actually said by Jesus. It also has to be realised that phrases like 'the son of God' which to a Jew could just mean a holy person takes on a different meaning when translated into Greek.

Books of criticism that I particularly like are those by Geza Vermes. He is a Jewish scholar. In particular his book *The Changing Faces of Jesus*[11] traces back the divine Jesus of St John's gospel to the Jesus of the synoptic gospels, and then to Jesus the man as he in fact was, a charismatic prophetic preacher. Jesus' teaching had a sublimity, and originality but that does not make him divine. Needless to say he still remains a man 'the latchet of whose shoe one is not worthy to unloose'.

One can see how the traditional Christian doctrine of the Incarnation and Holy Trinity developed, by believers over the centuries. As for the doctrine of the Atonement, I feel this was largely invented by St Paul. He had never met Jesus and in his letters there is virtually nothing about Jesus' ministry. He deals almost exclusively with Jesus' death and resurrection. He interprets these as necessary events that reversed the Fall and enabled man to be reunited with God. Yet as far as one can see from the synoptic gospels, in Jesus' actual ministry there was none of this. Jesus summons people to follow him and come to God at once. It in no way depends upon his death.

I am left with the mystery of what actually convinced the disciples of the resurrection. I continue to search for a completely convincing natural explanation. The first account of it is that of Paul on the road to Damascus. There was no bodily presence but a bright light and voice which according to one of the accounts was an inner voice not heard by those with him. Peter may have had a similar experience. These and similar experiences may have been converted into bodily resurrection stories. Matthew 27: 2-3 show how congenial and readily believable bodily resurrection stories were at the time.

---

11 Geza Vermes, *The Changing Faces of Jesus* (Allen Lane, London 2000). Paperback edition published by Penguin in 2001.

Another book I found startling is *After Christianity*[12] by Daphne Hampson. She points out that Judaism and Christianity are fundamentally male constructions. She claims that no woman could possibly have conceived of a God as he is portrayed in both the Old and the New Testaments. Her second great point is that Christianity involves a belief in a particular and unique intervention into history from outside. This is an untenable belief in the modern world with its scientific knowledge and attitudes.

We are left with the question: does God exist and if so what is his nature? At the moment everyone is thinking of Darwin, as it is 150 years since the publication of *The Origin of Species*. I fully accept evolution and Darwin's theory has been fully confirmed by the discovery of DNA. Evolution is compatible with Deism but what is the nature of a God who creates a world that for millions of years has progressed by survival of the fittest? Not I think a God of Love.

As we think of the origin of the universe, we are left with many questions to which we do not and probably never will know the answer. I like the conclusion of Bryan Magee in his book *Confessions of a Philosopher*.[13] He says 'What I want to see are two mass migrations, one out of the shallows of rational humanism to an appreciation of the mystery of things, the other out of religious faith to a true appreciation of our ignorance'.

Despite all I have written I still regularly attend church. The church provides an excellent community and every church I have known contains wonderful people, who do so much good in the world. I may not accept the doctrine of the church but the moral teaching of Jesus is marvellous. The weakness of the books by Dawkins and Hitchens that attack religious belief is that they concentrate on the evil that religious belief has caused in the world but say nothing of the immense good the Christian faith has inspired.

---

12 Daphne Hampson, *After Christianity* (SCM Press, London 1996).
13 Bryan Magee, *Confessions of a Philosopher* (Weidenfeld and Nicholson, London 1997).

I do not want to undermine anyone's faith or upset relatives or other clergy who hold traditional beliefs. And for this reason I wish to maintain anonymity. In the Christmas story I love the wise men who follow a star. I feel we should all follow the star of truth in so far as we can, and so I have the nerve to sign myself

Magus Minor

A Busy Decade

Penny Mawdsley

I have always experienced life as a creative activity. Sometimes I feel that it is like remodelling a ball of clay to shape it for ever-changing requirements. At other times it seems more akin to weaving a length of fabric whose pattern becomes more complex as new shades and textures are introduced into it. But more prosaically perhaps, I most often find it like being faced with bowls of disparate 'use-ups' at the back of the fridge and knowing that somehow I have to turn them into an appetising meal. I've found within the SOF Network the encouragement to continue to look at life's creative potential and I hope that I'm becoming more appreciative of the many things that at first seem to get in the way of my continually revised 'grand vision' for the future. I see them as an important part of life itself.

In attempting to continue the autobiographical exercise that I began a decade ago for a chapter in *This is My Story*[14] I find myself unpacking the wording of the title to this volume, *This Life on Earth*. I'm opting here to take 'This life' as *my* life – as *I* reflect upon it – *my* life with *my* subjective interpretation, given *my* spin. It will be *this* life rather than *that* life, the one I might have had. Indeed I see the task before me as an attempt to give some coherence to the unfolding catalogue of choices I have made and actions I have taken, or have failed to take, in the past and within the context of my particular given background. Incidentally, I am conscious, as someone born in the West in the middle of the twentieth century, albeit into a practising Christian family, that I never saw *this life* as a mere preparation for any sort of everlasting *life to come*, as might have been the case had I been born a century earlier.

---

14 *This is My Story,* edited by Teresa Wallace (Sea of Faith Network, 1998).

Even given exactly the same opportunities (and limitations) that my particular home background, my education, natural ability, personality and chance encounters have provided, the *that life* I might have had is for me, if not for anyone else, a fascinating subject for speculation. I concede of course that to contemplate what I might have been or achieved would be a thoroughly fruitless exercise. I therefore intend that my contribution to *This Life on Earth* will consist of my recalling some highlights from the last ten years and briefly reflecting on them. Before I launch into such an account, however, I should conclude the 'unpacking' exercise with what some might regard as a facetious observation sparked off by the phrase *on Earth* at the end of the title.

Writing in my 60th year on this precious planet I confess to a sense of great relief that the global population explosion, food shortages and technological advances haven't yet forced me to leave my terrestrial home! Despite growing up at the height of the 'Space Race', I have always found outer space terrifying, albeit utterly fascinating, and I have never harboured any ambition to travel outside the Earth's atmosphere. My imagination, even when I let it fly unfettered, is somehow always grounded in my personal – mundane – experience of life. The worlds of Fantasy Realism and Sci-Fi usually leave me cold.

The last decade has been a busy one for me, in which many things have *happened,* to which I have needed to respond and also one in which I have consciously initiated action. I'm glad to have come through it alive, though how unscathed by my experiences it is not easy for me to judge. On Trinity Sunday 1998, I finally lost patience with the Church and left it, not to darken its doors since, except to attend rites of passage for friends and relatives. The loss is mine entirely: atmospheric buildings, familiar music, magnificent prose from the Golden Age of English Literature, to say nothing of supportive church friends acquired down the years. I miss them all but I can no longer cope with all those other aspects that orthodox Christianity and church attendance unfortunately require.

In 2006 I joined the British Humanist Association and its affiliated local outpost in Chester, where I am now serving as its Social Secretary and its representative on the Chester Interfaith Forum. Through the latter I have joined the Harmony Project, which is working for community cohesion in the area. This entails visits to local schools to introduce the children to a Humanist alternative to the belief systems and practices offered by my fellow Harmony Project members. Chester Humanists feel proud that we have been included in the project. Richard Johnson, a fellow Humanist and SOF member, is responsible for building up that vital trust and rapport necessary to enable us to work successfully alongside the local faith groups.

On the family front there has been plenty going on over the last decade, which has involved me to a greater or lesser extent. Indeed the family scene has not been without its traumas during that time. These have included the death of my mother in autumn 2000. For the previous eight years, since my father's death, I had been travelling up weekly to Cumbria to help her with business and household matters. She died leaving a large house and adjoining cottage, both stuffed full of family detritus – some valuable, most not – which had accumulated over the previous century and a half, and which had come up intact with my parents when they moved north from Surrey twenty years before. Clearing out the cellars and outhouses, let alone the rest of both residences, was a nightmare, albeit one with fascinating lighter moments, that lasted for nine months.

The enormity of the enterprise can be measured in terms of the two large pantechnicons filled with furniture and miscellanea destined for the sale rooms, along with three charity white vans and a large house-clearance collecting truck. Shortly before the house and cottage went on the market, a Saturday was put aside for a grand in-house jumble sale, which made £1000 for the church and village school. We made 29 trips to the council tip (a 40 minute round trip away) with car and trailer stuffed to the gunnels before the final dramatic act, the auction of both properties in the village hall. That was some year! My sister and I readily acknowledge that we would never have come through the experience without my husband's expert supervision and practical help, to say nothing of many a glass of sherry and box of *Pringles* at the end of each long day!

Spanning the last decade, both children have moved out of the family home, graduated, one from Cambridge, the other from Central St. Martin's and King's London respectively. Gareth passed out from Dartmouth and after serving briefly in the Gulf has worked in various logistical jobs for the Royal Navy including at the Ministry of Defence. Katy did a PGCE and is now teaching history and philosophy at a girls' school in Cheshire. We learned to cope with 'Empty Nest Syndrome' – and the need to assimilate Gareth's early marriage and his symbolic *final* departure from the family home.

The next event of note was sparked off by my husband's retirement, shortly after which we prepared to move from our home in north Liverpool where we had lived for 23 years to Bodfari, a village near Denbigh. This involved a three months' winter sojourn in a log cabin in a remote part of West Wales while we hunted for a new house after selling up in Blundellsands. The last three years have been spent settling into our new locality, making friends and planting a garden in a former quarry yard.

More recent challenging experiences for me were associated closely with the life of SOF Network. The first was my year (2006-2007) as Chair of the SOF Trust, a stressful and unhappy one for me and for the members amongst whom I spread unmitigated doom and gloom. I followed this by an anxious year as organiser of the 2008 annual conference in Liverpool, which thankfully turned out well and was apparently enjoyed by the majority of those who came.

Somehow, other more typical midlife experiences of the last decade have been accommodated alongside everything else. I'm thinking here of things like the menopause (which in my case led to severe alopecia); of supporting my husband's transition into active retirement and my sister's move from New Zealand to Edinburgh – and so on, to say nothing of the delight and responsibility of becoming a grandmother. It is astonishing to me, looking back, that we managed to keep going with day-to-day chores at the same time as trying to sort and pack up our own family home prior to the move to Wales, and looking after a succession of elderly family friends whose needs demanded an ever-increasing amount of our time and energy. And this is to ignore the requirement of being on hand to organise the usual family feasts and festivals (including 18th, 21st and 50th birthday parties, as well as a big silver wedding 'do', which neatly combined celebrations for Gareth's engagement and Katy's A-Level results.).

What of course is missing from this list is an entry for 'Work', an important component of most people's lives! I haven't taken paid employment (apart from a month's worth of part-time supply teaching) since Gareth's birth thirty years ago. Where is the tick against the 'Charity work' box to plug the erstwhile 'Church Activities' gap? There isn't one. SOF has been my charity work at both national and local level. There are other apparent glaring omissions: 'Sport' and 'Leisure Pursuits'. Although I've gradually been making good the latter since our move, I still haven't managed to fit in the regular country walking, to which I aspire and which would be very good for me. I find myself only making the effort when we have visitors staying.

What has happened to my earlier political activism? The 1974 October General Election, at which I stood for Bessie Braddock's old seat, Liverpool Scotland Exchange, seems a lifetime away. I haven't dismissed the idea of standing one day for our local community council (despite its ridiculously low budget and consequent lack of real clout), but I can't find the time at the moment. I've signed petitions about this and that, but not gone on any public demonstrations.

What do I think about the Big Issues? I believe it makes sense to do all we can individually, nationally and internationally to preserve biodiversity and to conserve the world's natural resources. I also believe that we should face up to the real possibility that humanity will sooner rather than later bring about its own extinction (as a result of excessive population growth, a fight for scarce food, water and energy supplies, greed, corruption, political apathy and disengagement leading to outbreaks of bio-, chemical and nuclear war). Such an unthinkable catastrophe might well be of benefit to the planet as a whole, allowing perhaps for the future evolution of another (more) intelligent and self-conscious species.

Very reluctantly I hold the pessimistic opinion that the alleviation of poverty, of providing adequate education and health care for all, along with adequate food, water and sustainable energy supplies, and access to justice and the rule of law, will never be anything like fully achieved, and certainly not without the need for armed conflict. I wish it were otherwise. If only we could somehow start with a clean slate! On the one hand, there would need to be a total elimination of corruption, self-seeking and greed at every level of society, and on the other, there would need to be a massive and sustainable injection of energy, courage and political will, if the world's leaders and bureaucrats were to make the necessary momentous changes required to bring about a safer, fairer and happier world for everyone.

Still Hankering

John Theodore Cragg

As a twelve year old boy I went to Christchurch, Blackpool with my auntie, as my own family had gone back to the USA. It was thoroughly low-church and I used to while away the service imagining I was a monkey able to leap among the roof-beams. Chapel at school was also lacking in ceremonial but I used to enjoy staying behind after the service to hear the organist practising. The section of the chapel where the younger boys sat was an extension forming a war-memorial transept, whose walls were covered with the names of old boys killed in the First World War. I have always since had a fascination for war memorials, although a friend told me she finds them oppressive.

When I reached university I discovered ritualism, beautiful singing and vestments, and thought it a great improvement on the style of worship I was used to. Perhaps I was attracted simply because it was a change; there was certainly an element of release from some kind of tyranny. I have also explained this to myself by noticing that priests of a catholic persuasion have a more ironical approach to morality. People who claim to be acting in God's name often seem to think that they are as perfect as He is and the Anglican Franciscans I met were not like this.

I became interested in becoming a monk myself and bought a book of monastic day hours, only to find I could not find my way round it. After reading *The Seven Storey Mountain*[15] and *The Sign of Jonas*,[16] I decided I really loved Thomas Merton and wanted my life to have the meaning his had. However, when I went to an Anglican theological college for an interview, the superior shone his anglepoise lamp in my face and asked what made me think

---

15 Thomas Merton, *The Seven Storey Mountain* was first published 1948.
16 Thomas Merton, *The Sign of Jonas* was first published in 1953.

God wanted me to be a priest. I did not have the appropriate answer.

I did not establish myself in any church congregation after leaving university but I still enjoyed reading the diaries of Thomas Merton, and after some years a friend introduced me to the Buddhist Society, who seemed to regard Merton as one of them. Zen training was tough and I did not have a strong grasp of it, as I do not enjoy reading technical religious works. But the atmosphere was different from Christianity and brought a release from its negative aspects.

When the novelty had worn away, I started to develop a sneaking suspicion that the toughness of the training was unnecessary in my case, as I had already undergone a tough Christian training. After leaving the Buddhists I still hankered after meditation and retreats, I am not sure why. I would not like to think the Hound of Heaven is pursuing me. The concept of conversion is troublesome; I admire the monastic ideal of conversion of morals but not the idea of suddenly being saved.

Anyway I have taken up Christian meditation but maintain identification with Buddhism. A friend warned me about meditation and it is difficult. On the other hand I felt disappointed when another friend said 'I don't meditate' as I think meditation is a good way of finding out what is going on in our subconscious. Basically, I want to agree with Freud that religion is a neurosis; but my father is a clergyperson and this has given me a strong streak, perish the thought, of religious conservatism.

Here is a poem by Basavanna from *Speaking of Siva:*[17]

---

17 Speaking of Siva, poems dedicated to Siva translated and introduced by AK Ramanujan (Penguin, London 1973). Reprinted as a Penguin Classic in 2006.

John Theodore Cragg

He'll grind till you're fine and small,
He'll file till your colour shows.
If your grain grows fine
in the grinding,
if you show colour
in the filing,
then our Lord of the Meeting Rivers
will love you
and look after you.

The Scent of the Roses

Peter Bellenes

On a recent visit to Brittany I wondered, as I wandered around the fading ill-attended churches, what had brought me, an Anglican priest in the year of my 60th birthday, thus far along a varied path of religious discovery. A member of SOF who started the journey of faith as a cradle Roman Catholic, my beliefs were formed in my early years by the fervent attentions of my godparents. These wonderful godparents ensured I went to mass and benediction every Sunday and made my novenas to the Black Madonna on Thursdays. The attentions of my godparents were not unwelcome, for they were a very kind and generous uncle and aunt, and church was accompanied by frequent visits to tea shops and other indulgences! My godparents were thrown into especially high relief as my mother was a Catholic who had been excommunicated automatically by marriage in a registrar's office.

My father was a non-believing socialist, antagonistic to all things religious, and so my early days were far from tranquil as my mother's extended family fought him for possession of my soul! I would return from church to be assailed by my father's barbs about all that 'Ace, Queen, King, Jack stuff'. I attended a county primary school, round 2 to dad, round 1 having been won by the family with baptism and church attendance. Round 3 also was won by the family as I was enrolled in a Catholic direct grant grammar school, from which I went into the seminary first in Aberystwyth and then in Salamanca. I left the seminary shortly after the famous encyclical on birth control *Humanae Vitae* and, on returning to England, qualified as a social worker. It was entering into a relationship with the woman who was to become my wife that led to radical changes in my outlook. My beloved would merely ask simple questions of my faith position, wanting to know more and forcing me to think things through to answer her. This made me more and more unsettled in my previously seemingly secure position.

On a visit to Lichfield Cathedral I bought Stephen Neill's book on Anglicanism and here I thought I had a found a Church open to enquiry, though my theology was still very conservative and was so when I was accepted for theological training at Lincoln. As the flood waters of Lincoln's radical protestant theology engulfed me I strove to anchor myself in the old ways. It was only on leaving Lincoln that I realised how much I had changed and what new perspectives I had taken on board and made my own. Since those heady days, almost thirty years ago now, I have continued to read, and question and, I hope, grow. The island of faith on which I now reside is in one sense seemingly small though, as a universalist, it is also much larger than the theological fortress I once imagined to be my home.

Strangely as someone who now sees all religion as a human construct, I still find myself possessed of a melancholy nostalgia. I go on retreat but always to Catholic monasteries and I attend mass on the continent and spent my sabbatical with Benedictine nuns in the USA. There is still something that haunts me as I wander though the places which, despite the many changes in Roman Catholicism, echo still to the music of past rites and religious observances. I bring to mind lines from the poem by Thomas Moore (1780-1852), *Farewell! But Whenever You Welcome The Hour:*

> Let Fate do her worst, there are relics of joy,
> Bright dreams of the past, which she cannot destroy;
> Which come, in the night-time of sorrow and care,
> And bring back the features that joy us'd to wear.
> Long, long be my heart with such memories fill'd!
> Like the vase in which roses have once been distill'd
> You may break, you may ruin the vase if you will,
> But the scent of the roses will hang round it still.

Will You Still Love Me Tomorrow?

Trevor Greenfield

Call me Pilgrim. It has a certain connotation. It presents an image of someone walking to somewhere in quiet unassuming certainty that the journey upon which they have embarked is more significant than the destination. Enigmatic and alone, at one and the same time both social and anti-social, an apotheosis of contradiction. I am a spiritual gunslinger, like Clint Eastwood in *Pale Rider*, except I have a Bible in one holster and the Bhagavad Gita in the other and I'm probably a little more handsome.

That's how the image presents itself to me, but if nothing else I'm nobody's fool and I know that *Call me Pilgrim* offers something else to my fragile self-perception – the smug satisfaction that derives from knowing that only people who have read *Moby Dick*, or at least the first sentence, will get the carefully crafted allusion to the painful, disturbing but sometimes insightful and happy journey upon which we all embark from womb to crematorium; *fragments I have shored against my ruins*, as T.S. Eliot would have it. *Christ, Trevor, you're such an arse*, as my friends would have it.

The crematorium is, perhaps, quite a good place to start if you want to know something about me. The physical remains of twenty-five percent of the people I have ever unconditionally loved and maybe forty percent of everyone I've felt some form of connection with ended up there; quite where the rest of their remains are now, assuming there are any other remains, is a question for another time.

I am not Everyman, I'm Ordinaryman, a wife, three kids, a dog and a weekly trip to Tesco; such are the idylls of my life. I have an average income, an average car, and an average existence. Oh, I nearly forgot, and an unrelenting desire to know about God, to understand death, and to find out what's real. Like I said, an average existence, but average is good. There is alchemy in average, the distillation of reality from the confusion of children's tears and the words of dying parents. There is potential and transformation in average, the world in a grain of sand. Well, maybe, let's hope so anyway, it's what we have.

When I was five I started going to Sunday school. When I was six I stopped going to Sunday school. Apart from standing in class at the end of each day with my hands together and eyes closed whilst muttering something about *trespasses,* that was as far as I got with organised religion for the next quarter century.

Hell played a formative part in my early years. Nobody threatened me with it; I just seemed to push it upon myself. Aged eight I would play in the local park whilst wondering if I'd go to Hell. My eldest daughter, aged 12, asked me recently if you go to Hell for telling lies. I was surprised to find Hell still on the agenda and happy to explain that no such place exists and that sometimes lies are good things. Hopefully she won't be subject to the vague uneasiness that lasted through my teenage years. I wasn't a God-botherer but I saw every temptation, from illicit sex to hard drugs, not as experiment or opportunity, but as a veering off the pilgrim path to a place you didn't want to spend eternity. Thinking back, I guess there are benefits to the concept of Hell. I never took heroin and I never got the clap, although it seems alien to me now to imagine that an Old Man in the Sky (and a seemingly kind Old Man at that) would look down at what I was doing and pitch-fork me into a furnace for such peculiar indiscretions. Surely he'd have better things to do. *God's not watching Felicity, trust me.*

My adult life was college, University reading Religious Studies and English, love, courtship and marriage, children and a series of jobs not really worth the doing. For a couple of years I ended up in Church, trying to fit what I believed to a dying theology. You know when you recite the Creed every Sunday… well, if you could replace *I believe in…* with *I'm trying believe in…* or even *I'd really like to believe in…* I'd probably still be there.

So, there you are, my adult life asked and answered in swift refrain because I'm leading you to your point of recognition. They were talking on Radio Four, two godless vicars and a bemused interviewer, about the *Sea of Faith*. They were explaining how things are either real or not real or, here's the good bit, non-real (why have two definitions to explain reality when you can have three!). I sent off for details. It seemed to me then, and still does, like an organisation for people who don't know what it is they don't believe in, and despite professing to have no interest in whatever it is they don't believe in, insist on talking about it at enormous length! Some of the poor bastards are even compelled to write books about it! Well, what can I say… it was like coming home! In fact, poor bastard that I am, I even wrote a book about it![18]

But in the end, when push comes to shove, I have a confession… I am a SOF member who believes in the existence of God. Not the Christian Gods: Yahweh, blundering through history slaughtering the first-born, all that benign anger and pent up frustration. Not Jesus, wandering through Palestine calming the raging storm that his Dad had probably just whipped up. Not the Holy Spirit, which, so far as I can tell, is a cross between a cloud and a ghost and I can't get passionate about either of those possibilities. Not Allah, because he doesn't appear to like dogs and I love dogs – besides which what could possibly be the point in being all-powerful and creating a species of animal you don't even like? Not Krishna, *destroyer of worlds,* or the remote, austere Brahma. I could continue but I'm sure you get the point.

My God is a necessity; someone or something that you have to build into your understanding of the Universe to make the most sense of it. Descartes would be proud of me. The Universe works O.K. without building in the concept of God but works even better if you do build it in. God or Darwin, I choose both. No Pascal's Wager here, honestly what a ridiculous proposition, I don't know how these people even get published! And none of

---

18 *An Introduction to Radical Theology* (O Books, Winchester 2006).

Dawkins' desire to reduce everything to biological impulse. Yes, there is tooth and claw savagery in the killing zones but there is spirit as well in this world, pulsing through the rhythm of the seasons, in sunrise and sunset, in the sacrifice of the antelope and in the love that passes between us. And it is greater than the sum of its parts.

The only question left to answer, I guess, is how you relate to a necessity, if indeed relation is necessary, or even the point. The answer, I suppose, is you relate here and now, during and through this life on Earth. Make choices and assumptions as you glimpse into the mirror. Faith or doubt, question or answer… it doesn't matter how it falls; they are two faces of the same coin. *Know the place for the first time* as Eliot would have it. *God's just a dream, Trevor, like world peace or a cure for cancer*, as my friends would have it. *I am a pilgrim on a journey*, as I would have it; a theist in SOF. Will you still love me tomorrow?

A Sense of Self

What on Earth is reality and who am I?

Bobbie Stephens Wright

What kind of person would spend years of a life asking the above questions, rather than taking reality for granted and moving onto the more valuable question what might I do in this life? Sadly I must report that I am the person who for some years was compelled to question both reality and my sense of selfhood. The reason for this is the story that I am about to tell of confusions that began very early in life and continued until I was over 40 years of age.

The story begins with my being born into a home where one parent had been reared as a Spiritualist (Mother) and the other as a pragmatic Marxist atheist, who lived for the day (Father). Yes, you may well wonder how these two ever got together: one believing that the real life was in the hereafter and this life was hell, a pessimist to the core; the other living in the moment as far as is humanly possible, an optimistic pragmatist.

I'd like to convey to my readers that some steady sense of reality and personhood were not part of my understanding for the first half of my life. Quickly inculcated into language, I was presented with two versions of reality. It will become apparent, no doubt, in the course of this story, that I am more attracted by Freudian psychoanalysis than by Jungian psychotherapy. However, I seem to have followed Jung's theory that it is in the second half of life that we begin to become concerned with spirituality and that we feel a need to work out problems inherent in our history. Ironically enough, I also share with Jung the experience of having a mother who was a Spiritualist. What I cannot share with him is the view that: 'I know' there is a God.

As an under-5 I attended the Sunday School at the local Methodist Church, my grandmother's former faith. I marvelled at the miracles of Jesus and lovingly placed the stamps I was given bearing his image into my stamp book. This I eventually grew away from but then later, as a Grammar School pupil, I attended the Anglican Church with my peer group, who were by then about to become confirmed in the Anglican tradition. My father, to whom all religion was anathema, although bemused, saw to it that I was up early on Sunday mornings and ready to attend church, where I was taken by my friend's kind and well-intentioned parents, who were equally bemused by this caring father who was an atheist and worse – a Marxist.

I decided for myself that I would join my peer group and become confirmed and my mother duly instructed a friend to make a suitable dress for me. Then came the final bible class before the actual confirmation and things began to change. The vicar looked me right in the eye and told me that God knew everything I thought, said and did. I looked back at him and thought that was quite ridiculous. It seemed that my father's daughter at 12 years was suddenly born. My friend and I passed through the huge double door of the Vicarage that night and I told her that I would not be confirmed. She asked me why and I told her I did not believe what the vicar had said.

Although the real problems with my identity and sense of self were not to occur till I was 35, there were pointers that there was something amiss in my psychological makeup. My mother had returned to work as a night nurse when I was six years old, primarily because my father, who was self-employed, had become bankrupt through no real fault of his own. We lost many of the trappings of life; the car went and even the telephone, which was considered a luxury in 1953. From having been very sociable and outgoing I became shy and withdrawn, having had impressed upon me by my mother and her family the disgrace he had brought upon us. I began to dislike school immensely and the teacher, who told mother of my great potential, asked that mother come to see the headmaster. Mother stood her ground and said that she now had to work because of the financial situation. She had elected to work at nights and so my brother and I did not see her at night and she was in bed during the day. She even elected to work at weekends and it took us till we were adults to work out that she was not so much avoiding us as she was our father, and especially at nights.

A string of sympathetic and wonderful teachers and friends saw me through childhood, difficult though I was, withdrawn, rebellious and strong-willed. On the other hand, there were odd displays of strange talents: veridical dreams and outstanding instances of *déjà-vu*. My friend of old still tells of how I saw her struggling in the sea with one of our mutual friends and was able to set the scene really accurately. A few years later this occurred exactly as I had predicted and she told me how she thought that she was quickly able to react when she suddenly remembered the warning I had given, which alerted her to the situation. I harboured the thought, probably because my mother worked in a Psychiatric Hospital, that I was quite barmy really.

This may even have been the reason that, when encouraged to join her profession, I actually worked as a student nurse in a psychiatric hospital. I understand rather better now why this led to me becoming very physically ill. I began to suffer from Ankylosing Spondylitis, which was to remain undiagnosed for 15 years, because it was thought in those days only to occur in men. I suffered psychologically because the whole ethos of the Psychiatric Hospital upset me. People herded like sheep, without their own clothes or possessions. Grandmothers with dementia sitting among dangerous psychotically ill patients. All patients hauled out of bed (including the elderly, in fact, especially the elderly), to be up and dressed by the time the day shift arrived at 7.30am. I particularly remember bath days, when patients had to share the water, which was neither clean nor warm, winter and summer alike. In those days I was tempted to say there but for the grace of God go I, but there was no evidence in the situation of a loving God who cared for all.

By the time I was in my twenties I had left the hospital and worked in finance for British Telecom. My mobility problems had worsened considerably and I was told that I would probably be in a wheelchair by the time I was 30. Fortunately, the bones at the bottom of my back fused together, through neglect rather than any medical intervention, and I did get some relief but was often completely disabled through bi-lateral sciatica. At 32 years, the illness was diagnosed and also declared incurable. Only certain exercises and drugs could help me. Neither proved particularly effective and the mobility issues continued. Then the fun really began. An appointment was made for me by my mother with a spiritual healer. Very much against the grain, I attended and had a prolonged ecstatic experience, which was to change the course of my life. I experienced the feeling of being surrounded by people who understood me completely. I walked in as an ill woman with mobility problems and left, not cured, but far more able-bodied and with the strange and forceful gift of an intuitive or clairvoyant. Having been told that I had been treated by discarnate beings and smiled upon by God, for a number of years I had no other way of understanding what happened that November night in 1982.

This eventually led to me working as a medium in the Spiritualist Church, where I soon began to show myself as difficult. I could do the job but declared that there were no guides. I was uncertain about the stories that Spiritualists told. They were not charlatans, because they apparently believed in spirits and a spirit world. I eventually became a threat to the hierarchy, who knew I was a sought-after clairvoyant but also that I did not buy into their beliefs. I eventually decided that I must leave the church because, although I thought the adherents were gullible, they were also vulnerable. I could not be responsible for eroding the belief systems of elderly folk who were nearing the end of their lives.

This departure did not occur before I was invited to demonstrate at the headquarters of the Spiritualists' National

Union, Stansted Hall, the SNU being recognised as the largest group of Spiritualists in Great Britain. Stansted Hall attracts an international audience, who usually visit to have their beliefs in life after death affirmed. I was lucky that on this occasion a psychoanalyst from Germany, Dr. Dietmut Niedecken attended, who had come to begin her research of 'the occult' through psychoanalytic theory. Apart from being impressed by my performance, she gathered that I was not popular with the regular mediums and that I seemed to reach psychological depths which were rather different from the banal information offered to the audience by the other 'mediums'.

Dr Niedecken approached me with the idea that she would invite me to Germany to demonstrate to some of her professional colleagues, and that in so doing, she would get to know me as a person and try to understand my psychological makeup. I was not keen to do the workshops in Germany, which were arranged on my behalf, because by this time years of dissociation had left me lacking stability as a person. I suffered bouts of depersonalisation, which ironically could only be assuaged by my performances as a clairvoyant. However, desperate to change this without really knowing how, I agreed to do the workshops. The mutual exchange between this group of professionals and myself eventually allowed me to reframe my experiences as a clairvoyant in the terms of psychoanalytic theory. For instance, when Dr. Niedecken asked me how I felt in the altered state of consciousness, or dissociation as I came to know it, I said it felt like me but not me. I was quickly introduced to the work of analyst D.W. Winnicott *Home is Where We Start From,* [19] where I discovered 'not me' was a term used in psychoanalytic theory that appeared in his discussion of infant-mother interrelationships. At last I had the means of understanding my experiences in different terms. I would eventually come to read Susanne Langer and appreciate her view that:

---

19 D. W. Winnicott, *Home is Where We Start From* (Norton, New York 1990).

> The formulation of experience which is contained within the intellectual horizon of an age and a society is determined, I believe, not so much by events and desires, as by the *basic concepts* at people's disposal for analysing and describing their adventures to their own understanding.[20]

For better or worse, human beings bear a burden, which purely alert creatures do not bear – the burden of understanding. Human beings live in time but also in history; they must come to conceive a world and the laws of the world. They must find a pattern of life and a way of meeting death. It becomes relatively easy to cope with the mundane, but as Langer also observed, the greatest fright of human beings is to meet what they cannot easily construe, the 'uncanny' as it is often called. The conception of such experiences is often thought to escape and elude everyday language.

Within the language of psychoanalytic theory, I became able to understand my habit of dissociation as a form of psychological defence mechanism. Long ago the well known medium Eileen Garrett was describing her trance states as self-hypnotic and describing the way in which she could just yawn herself out of existence. The American analyst and writer Nancy McWilliams describes such personalities in the following way:

> People who use dissociation as their primary defence mechanism are essentially virtuosos in self-hypnosis. Movement into an altered state of consciousness when one is distressed is not possible for everybody; you have to have the talent.[21]

---

20 Susanne K. Langer, *Philosophy in a New Key: A Study in the Symbolism of Reason, Rite, and Art* (Third Edition: Harvard University Press, Cambridge, Massachusetts 1996), page 6.
21 Nancy McWilliams, *Psychoanalytic Diagnosis: Understanding Personality Structure in the Clinical Process* (The Guilford Press, New York 1994), page 328.

Having already begun to seek out the side of my personality that Jung would refer to as 'the shadow', I read in McWilliams that the most recurrent theme in psychoanalytic literature on narcissism shows that the people at risk of developing a narcissistic character may be constitutionally more sensitive than others to unverbalised emotional messages. All of this was useful to the role of a clairvoyant but not to the development of a mature adult personality. Although a painful process, I believe it is better to become aware of one's failings and accepting of one's limitations.

    I am reminded here of the Editorial of *Sofia* magazine for July 2005, in which our editor Dinah said that she had always been puzzled at the postmodernist idea that we do not have a self or identity but are many selves, many identities. Dinah said that this was not her experience at all, that she had always felt herself to be herself as far back as she could remember. I told Dinah privately that she was lucky that she had always enjoyed such a secure sense of herself. The work of psychoanalysts such as Donald Winnicott and, more latterly, Nancy McWilliams reveals that this secure sense of self is not available to all human beings, and that psychological disintegration and depersonalisation are perhaps more common than we think. Psychoanalysis may not provide definitive answers to the occult but it does provide a theory in which such things can be understood as fully human. The philosopher Thomas Nagel[22] writing as long ago as 1974 on consciousness in an article 'What is it like to be a bat?', showed an awareness of the difficulty of understanding the subjective experiences of another, but still maintained the hope that it should be possible to describe the subjective character of experience in a form comprehensible to beings incapable of having those experiences. My contention is that psychoanalysis, in particular, lends itself to the understanding of mediumship.

---

22 *Philosophical Review* 83: 435-50.

Now, Here

Ken Smith

I was much disturbed, many years ago, to read Samuel Beckett, in a plea for humanity, telling us that we had to learn to listen to the screams continually. Not an easy injunction to heed but one I've been much haunted by, with the result that, having given a huge amount of my working life, heart, mind, energy, to teaching the young about the hungry, the homeless, the elderly, the mad and marginal folk of all kinds, I now find myself content to spend much of what time remains to me, ministering to the dead and bereaved, the choking, screaming ones. I think my deepest emotion is, maybe always has been, a great and sometimes unbearable compassion welling up inside me. Blake's Pity with its human face, Dinah Livingstone's Kindness, that kins me to the entire Cosmos – in these days of belief and unbelief – are what I believe in, what makes me tick.

Sometimes I have made people smile with the observation 'he/she has a rich, inner life' – to describe the outwardly sad individuals who in increasing numbers walk the streets of our world talking to themselves (no, not the ones using their mobile phones). I didn't smile, however, yesterday on the London Tube when briefly, in company with others in the same compartment, I thought we might die at the hands of someone with a rucksack who started shouting threats at nobody in particular, telling them that they were going to (die – that is); but it re-enforced my understanding of the sometimes dangerous separateness of us all.

I think I have a rich, inner life too, and have been known to wander the streets, giving me an empathy with the sad, mad, and sometimes bad. People who know me well assure me (as I do myself) that I'm none of these. Even the depression that has, periodically, afflicted me over decades has receded – thanks to SOF, careful medication, good friends and common sense.

I have never lived so much in the present as I do now. Well, where else is there? I'm aware that my memory is not as sharp, my hopes, my ambitions for my future reduced, reshaped by the time I have left. But equally, never have I been so aware of other presents, other places, other people. I have been lucky and unlucky over the longish years of my life to have had friends, teachers, colleagues who have developed in me a sometimes painfully acute imagination. I learned for the first time as a young child – maybe from an Enid Blyton story-book – that there were things beyond sight, over the horizon of both my physical and my conscient world. I used to frighten myself with the immensity of space, the almost unimaginable aeons of time, the sometimes gross enormity of matter. I still find it difficult to gaze into the sky, without being overcome with a dread, an ache in the brain.

Though the despair and distortion of my psyche, brought about by chemotherapy, has left me now, I still find myself struggling with the ultimate futility of things. Fortunately, I've also learnt to foster the art of being gloriously alive in the present moment. Perhaps that's the secret – to hold together two thoughts, two feelings, even two opposites at the same time.

So how did I get to this state of affairs? My earliest introduction to Philosophy was via Bertrand Russell when I was in the Sixth Form. Three years later, Plato's *Republic* marked the beginning of my London BD in preparation for my ordination to the Anglican priesthood, but the evangelical nature of my college ensured that I left mouthing the scriptural injunction to prefer the foolishness of the Cross to the wisdom of the world. For a big part of my early adult life I was painfully conservative (not in politics – my Dad saw to that) but in all matters religious.

In 1954 I had been 'converted' by Dr Billy Graham – though he would have said I was 'saved' by the Grace of God, the Blood of the Lord Jesus and the indwelling of the Holy Spirit. Today my theology, like my philosophy, has trickled into the sand. But I want also to say that while the scars of my adolescent religious experience remain with me, those early years have enriched as well as shadowed my sense of who I am. I find that a lot of people can't seem to do that, can't revisit the past without bitterness, shame, regret. The sometimes contemptuous vehemence of the atheist/theist debate, of the non-realist/fundamentalist argument saddens me. It's a dualism that impoverishes, diminishes our humanity.

Strangely, though, I am still a Trinitarian. But now it is the Holy Trinity of space, time and stuff that draws my devotion. In more orthodox days, the Athanasian creed stated: 'Now this is the Catholic faith: We worship one God in Trinity and the Trinity in unity, without confusing the persons or dividing the substance; for the person of the Father is one, the Son's is another, the Holy Spirit's another; but the Godhead of the Father, Son, and Spirit is one, their glory equal, their majesty coeternal.' Perhaps something similar needs to be done with my modern secular equivalent. I'm sad that in the debate fuelled by conventional atheists, the sacredness of stuff doesn't get much of a look in. Maybe there is, at least for some of them, an element of anger (to quote Peter Cooke the comedian) that the bastard (God) doesn't exist. In today's concern for 'the environment' the same is also true. How humanly self-centred that word 'environment' is! Too much of it appears to be driven by fear, guilt and self-interest rather than a genuine respect for the Earth itself. The return of 'mother' imagery in some circles with regard to the Earth is nevertheless encouraging.

Personally I still want (even in my non-belief) to take my shoes off on the holy ground of existence. The pupils at my last school will recall that that was how I sometimes taught, barefoot on the grass near the rugby pitch (not on it – that would have been a different kind of sacrilege!). I still dip my fingers in holy water when I enter a church; I still touch the doorstep of the temple, gurdwara, or shrine before crossing the threshold. For me now, Space, Time, Stuff (or whatever words you prefer) are the only given. I'm totally content with them as the prerequisites for our existence. Especially as, with my increasing years, they intrude in their rawness and their demand to exercise their right, their hold over me. Of course, evolutionarily speaking, the plain truth is that in the beginning was the grunt – primeval. Everything else in our human world is secondary. In the beginning was the grunt. And the grunt became the word, the word became flesh and a specific set of words – my Dad saying to my Mum: 'Will you marry me?' – allowed me to be.

Two years ago, my illness trapped me at home for months and caused me to pass the time exploring the internet, the worldwide web. I went places I'd never been before. I did the RSPB survey on birds visiting my garden; I bought a new mattress online to ease my spine; in hope I booked a flight for a break on the continent. I used Wikipedia to plumb the depths of my ignorance. And then I began to ponder a deeper worldwide web, the one that will/can never be recorded – the entire human matrix, with its bookends of conception and birth, death and burial; and all the moments and places in between, the material that is the compulsive but elusive bread and butter of the media, the stuff for research that will continue to satisfy curiosity, continue to frustrate the seekers of others' wisdom, continue to give bad men opportunities to exercise control, have power over others.

Whilst I acknowledge the primacy of shared language into which we are born and bred, and which enables us to function in society; whilst I agree that there is no private language (we are all born into a part of the web of words, albeit only a fraction of the totality of linguistic symbols 'out there'), the reality of our everyday experience is the inwardness of the separate brain's function that gives rise to, and sustains, the individual me. Everything is inside the individual human brain. Therefore no conception, no brain; no brain, no consciousness; no consciousness, no language; no language, no meaning. It's true of all of us: we have a rich inner life.

I Was in the Fabled Black Book

Richard Hall

Being brought up by caring parents in the secure world of 1950s suburban Surrey, my older sister, Rosemary, and I were free to explore our little worlds. I dug to Australia in the back garden and on rainy days I constructed mechanical marvels from Meccano. My sister did whatever older girls did and, to my father's delight, learned to play the piano; so I resisted music. On Sundays we went to the Methodist Sunday School. I think my parents wanted an hour's peace and quiet after the Sunday roast but part of me believes they wanted to see us culturally educated, as there was no hint of religion on their part. When we said we didn't want to go any more there was no pressure to continue. I had joined the Boys' Brigade but the BB included monthly church parades, where I continued to absorb fragmentary Bible stories and Wesleyan hymns.

Sometime during those years I remember stunning my father with a question at Sunday tea as we munched our sandwiches, 'Daddy, what are people on Earth for?'

Now my father had a wonderful handlebar moustache and if he was about to say something good he was in the habit of twirling one end of it. He twirled.

'Well, son, we are put on this Earth to glorify God and enjoy him forever.'

I took this without comment but I could not square it with the rest of my father or mother. During his twirl Daddy had been dragging up memories of the Shorter Westminster Catechism from his strict Baptist upbringing. Daddy was a metallurgist working on classified material for the Ministry of Defence. It was about that time that he gave me the idea, then new to me, that he had discarded the religious beliefs of his parents since science had overtaken them but the morals were 'jolly good'. Later, at Tiffin Boys' School in Kingston-upon-Thames, there was morning chapel of hymn, reading, prayer, plus a weekly lesson of the much-derided Religious Instruction. I learnt little from them but to Daddy's delight I joined the school choir, which invariably sang religious works, so the drip-feed continued.

When I was 13, father, mother and I moved to the USA for three years. Sister Rosemary decided to stay in England as her O-level examinations were approaching and her music education was expanding. The move came because my father was offered a scientific-liaison post at the British Embassy in Washington DC. The colorful, Disney-world of 1958 America changed me from a middle-class British pudding to a string-bean transatlantic youth. At High School there was no chapel and no RI. I barely noticed their absence as the teen-oriented culture vibrated all around in and out of school.

Next door, on the corner of our Maryland bungalow, lived an elderly couple, Marge and Ralph, friends of my folks. In the summer I mowed their lawn for the going rate of $5. One Saturday I had finished mowing when a bronzed, dark-haired girl in blouse and shorts appeared. She lived on the other side of Marge and Ralph. I had glimpsed her from a distance and taken little notice but now, up close, she was lovely. She confidently introduced herself as Mary and after a moment stated her mission.

'Could you come over and help me with my algebra homework?'

Could I! She was a grade below me in school but I was a further year ahead because of my English education, and I was good at algebra thanks to Dad's tuition. I stowed the mower, hurdled the fence and solved the algebra. She was impressed. That week I went round several times to check on the progress of her math and within a week I had given my life to Mary. Then came her main mission. One evening, Mary fetched her Bible, not any Bible, but her Bible, well thumbed and annotated. She pointed out verses to me: verses that convict the ignorant of their sins, their need of a savior and salvation offered in the death of Jesus Christ. I was fifteen, and nothing, not Sunday School, not the Boys' Brigade, not even the Shorter Westminster Catechism had prepared me for the beautiful Mary witnessing to me in the warm basement of her home. Suddenly, I discovered religious America.

Mary's parents invited me to their church, Wallace Memorial Presbyterian, in Washington. It was built like a cinema with tiers of plush, tip-up seats. There was a vibrant Youth Group, into which I was accepted, but their evangelical conversation was horrific and enticing to my ears. One young man called Dale asked me if I liked the Kingston Trio, which was the great folk group of that era. My dad had bought me a guitar because I showed a glimmering of musical interest in buying every KT album. Dale pushed on, picking out one song from one album, which had the word 'damn' in it. I had barely noticed it but for Dale it condemned everything by the Kingston Trio. In spite of such trials, by the end of the summer I had given my life to Jesus – without ditching Mary, of course.

Again I had stunned my father but my parents did not try to talk me out of it. I'm sure they thought I'd grow out of it, but, without a hint of moustache twirling, my father bought me a copy of the new, New English Bible, New Testament, for my sixteenth birthday. They even supported my intention to become ordained after our return to England. I travelled with the Youth Group to hear Billy Graham in Philadelphia. I went forward and was put in touch with a counsellor with whom I corresponded for many months. Thankfully, it ceased, but my correspondence with the lovely Mary lasted a whole year before it, too, inevitably, faded.

Back at Tiffin School I knuckled down to O-levels. School also supplied minor persecution from old friends and older teachers, which convinced me I was on the right path.

Meanwhile, my father was found to be seriously ill. He rapidly declined and spent weeks being investigated in various hospitals. While mother and I were visiting him a nurse came in with a questionnaire. I remember only the last question, 'What religion are you?'

With difficulty my father raised himself on his pillow and twirled his moustache: 'Scientific humanist,' he replied.

Now I knew how Dad labelled his own position and the milieu in which Rosemary and I had been nurtured. The baffled nurse tried again.

'Is that sort of C of E?'

'That'll do,' Dad grinned. He collapsed on to his pillow and twirled his moustache for the last time.

I believed my father was now eternally condemned. It was autumn 1962. Dad knew Rosemary had passed her A-levels but not that I had passed my O-levels as he sank into unconsciousness and death. To my shame, I cannot remember feeling any great sorrow or remorse or pain.

As mother went out to work, Rosemary and I both insisted we should, too. Mother said no, Daddy would have wanted us to get all the education we could. We admitted he would. I began science A-levels with a view to reading Psychology at university followed by application to the Church of England ministry. *Honest to God*[23] had recently been published. I was challenged to a school debate and was pressed into opposing the book. It being the first semi-public opportunity to witness to my new belief I took it on. Being totally inexperienced at formal debating I was thrashed and humiliated. I decided that would never happen again.

My father's desire that we children should be musical now came to flower. Rosemary gained major qualifications for piano and organ and, with a couple of pals, I formed a folk trio at school – the Kingston-upon-Thames Trio – and after small

---

23 John A. T. Robinson, *Honest To God* (SCM Press, London 1963).

performances at local schools and clubs we found ourselves booked at Guildford Cathedral for the annual Easter Monday Youth Rally. We performed on the theme *From Cradle to Cross,* collecting all the songs we knew that would fit and writing others where there were gaps. Rosemary helped us with the production and I am sure Dad would have joined the thousands in the cathedral or on the hill.

Proceeding to University was a formality in 1965. I gravitated to the Evangelical Christian Union. Like my American Youth Group, it was throbbing with beautiful people, who spoke the language and were, apparently, living the life. A friend laid hands on me and I spoke in tongues. Sex, drugs and rock'n'roll were all around but we resisted such temptations except the rock'n'roll. With guitar in hand and with two other ECU friends, I formed another singing trio. We sang as part of the cabaret at a couple of college balls and were even thanked for our clean act. Intellectually, I was working through the nineteenth century science and religion issues, which were new to me. Some sharp edges began to be rubbed smooth and I became a little more tolerant, particularly of other shades of Christianity, but at the end of my first academic year the ECU President requested a private chat. I wondered what judgment was arriving as I felt evangelical guilt sweep in. In fact he invited me to be President the following year. However, it was 1967 and I remember almost nothing of my presidency during that great Summer of Love.

After graduation I had a frustrating hiatus awaiting training for ordination. For two years I worked in a Christian bookshop, which was a front for Brother Andrew and his colleagues who smuggled Bibles behind the iron curtain. It was a curious activity, packing parcels of books by day and tucking Bibles into hollow panels in an old Volkswagen camper after hours.

I was still an evangelical when I applied for training in the Church of England and I was not disappointed in expecting some confrontation. There was a sharp exchange with the Bishop who chaired my Selection Conference. He rudely quizzed me on

Matthew 27:52, 53 and I fell to the defensive. My debating skills must have improved since school as I learned to my surprise that I had been accepted for training. By contrast, my acceptance at Clifton Theological College was greeted with modest alacrity. In my time Clifton merged with Tyndale Hall and the women's college, Dalton House with St Michael's, to form Trinity College. Before the three merged I thought it would be a good plan to meet our fellow students socially. I approached the Principal suggesting a three-college dance. This was met with less alacrity.

'Richard', he said, 'dancing is a vertical expression of a horizontal desire.'

Such disappointment. Nonetheless, here, at Trinity, I knew I would learn the intellectual answers to become the fully equipped evangelical debater. That, too, proved a disappointment. During a New Testament seminar on Bultmann our tutor calmly informed us that we must keep a 'divided mind': learn the academic stuff to pass your exams but separate it from the Truth for the pulpit, the people and the parish. I am pleased to say all we students were shocked.

My curacy was at Holy Trinity, Eastbourne, evangelical cathedral of the south. In three years I conducted five weddings, five baptisms but 120 funerals. My naïve ambitions were not fulfilled. Dull worship had to be conducted, elderly women had to be visited but, worst of all, my finely honed addresses failed to have any effect. My vicar insisted on the 'divided mind' principle and I resented the refusal to share two hundred years of theology. All my intellectual questions rose again – that I thought had been answered – plus some new ones, notably the emerging medical-ethical issues, which new science and new laws were requiring us to debate. My one delight was that the youth club enjoyed working at these things. The final straw was that the vicar wanted me to play hymns on the guitar. I was 32 and I decided to quit. It sent the vicar onto his bed of sickness and me to Lewes for more sharp exchanges with a bishop. Conspicuously lacking was that much vaunted Christian compassion. Wrath and condemnation were to the forefront. My church colleagues and friends melted away. I experienced a second conversion into a new freedom.

Out of the church I was unemployed and homeless. It was left to an old university friend to pick me up in his van and take me in for the long, hot summer of 1976. Naturally, my first thought was, 'What can I do now?' I was neither educated nor trained for anything. The remote possibility was teaching Religious Education. I prepared a CV and wrote responses to every advertisement I saw. My degree was so old that it was still regarded as a teaching qualification but, to nobody's surprise, most of my applications gained refusals until a Headmaster with an idea opened my letter.

Stan Dixon's idea was that he attempted to hire teachers who had already been in a job related to their subject. I matched his idea and I was hired as assistant RE teacher at St John's Comprehensive, Epping. This was no learning curve; this was a cliff face. I knew nothing. I had no idea how to face thirty teenagers six times a day, who had no wish to be there learning religion, and my much-prized academic learning was of pitiful use. For three years, the last two lessons of every Friday afternoon ended in the hut on the far side of the playground with two successive Fifth year classes, who were simply out to taunt the teacher. I had one success: a boy approached me up the centre aisle with a homemade knife. I will never know his intention but with even less knowledge of self-defence I wrested the knife from his grip. I gained a little respect from the kids for about twenty minutes. There were moments of respite. I began a junior guitar group. As a newly-fledged teacher I believed I could teach a musical instrument. It filled many a lunch hour with the joy of seeing some eager students. I joined the school barbershop octet and occasional evenings were spent in great harmony. Best of all, I persuaded my Head of Department to let me start an A-level set. We had a most encouraging start with six students, all of whom enjoyed their studies and gained good grades. I am sure that helped my supervisor to pass me as a qualified teacher and recommend that I look for a Head of Department job.

At an interview in Cornwall I faced the Bishop of Truro. After a brief consultation with his chaplain, he faced me with my church departure. I was in the fabled Black Book. Clearly the interview was over and as I had no intention of wasting time I departed. A subsequent interview at King Edward VI School, Southampton, ended with success. So began a fruitful and contented 26 years. Although the job description required the Head of Religion also to be in charge of assemblies of the hymn, reading, prayer variety, I was soon able to slide the religious assemblies onto others. Syllabus changes took longer but over time world religions, philosophy and ethics were introduced, with every student taking GCSE Religious Studies and a healthy handful taking A-level Philosophy. Privately, I was moving to a non-realist position and it was wonderful to read *Taking Leave of God*[24] and find my own thoughts articulated. At Teachers' Masterclass conferences I questioned the omission of Cupitt from RE/Philosophy syllabuses. He was regarded as too avant-garde and, besides, syllabus content had stopped in the 1960s. I was aghast but the Don Cupitt canon was gradually added to the School library.

At the age of 48 I joined SOF: another sixteen-year conversion. At the age of 60 I retired, finding that I had generated 50 assembly talks that tracked Don Cupitt's ideas. The following year I discovered that we had taught most of Dawkins' *The God Delusion*[25] to our GCSE students, though in a less abrasive manner, to great examination success. This year I shall be 64 and my mind is free and easy as I work at the issues of our time; the Kingston-upon-Thames Trio has met up again and, if I had my dad's moustache, I'd twirl it.

---

24 Don Cupitt, *Taking Leave of God* (SCM Press, London 1980).
25 Richard Dawkins, *The God Delusion* (Houghton Mifflin, Boston 2006). Paperback edition with additions published by Black Swan in 2007.

Kindness is the Greatest Virtue

Joanna Clark

In the 1960s I went to Kings College, London to study Theology. At first I found it very difficult until I discovered the trick of jumping. It was assumed that there was a God and that we must study the 'Proofs of God' in order to learn to assess the correctness and errors in the proofs, not to assess the actual existence of God. But once I had learned how to jump, with the assumptions agreed, it was all plain sailing.

Not only did I sail happily, I even became part of the crew. Although I became a teacher, which always gave me the option of sitting outside all religions and looking at them with (I hope, for my pupils' sake) interest, gradually my private life became more church-connected. In the end I became a Reader (a lay preacher). Nevertheless, I remained a fairly heretical person, and joining SOF as soon as it began gave me a back-up which I sorely felt the need for.

Now that I am a retired person I feel beautifully free to do all the things old people can do – dress in purple and pink, drag my umbrella along railings, wear comfy, unfashionable shoes, not attend church services and best of all, not even try to accept any of the religious notions that I have tried so hard to swallow over the years.

This sounds negative, but in fact it is positive, for now I am positively free to develop my own ideas without feeling that I am being arrogant, presumptuous, or cooking up a mishmash. What is wrong with a mishmash anyway? In science and the arts it is regarded as creative to learn from others and to take on their discoveries to alter and enrich one's own. So – here is where I am now.

I am pretty sure that the world has no detailed purpose. Slates fall off roofs and hit, or miss, anyone who happens to be passing by. Viruses clobber young people as well as the old completely randomly. No one, no being, is planning for this. Even the way we react to such disasters is not a God-given (or fate-given) chance to learn, or to earn merit (or disgrace). Our reactions are our own; our will-power is based on our genes, our upbringing and the events. Maybe we can choose, a little, to learn and grow from the events, to make life more bearable for those around us, to sit light to the fragility of life. But there is no great plan.

I am sure there is no Fatherly care (Christian) or Compassionate and Merciful being (Islam), nor an all-knowing Law giver (Hinduism) for me. Miracles cannot happen – coincidences, ignorance, loving care, genetic variations, yes, but never God-given miracles.

I appreciate that for some people their religions give them access to a community, shared beliefs and security in the old traditions, but the actual beliefs and words of these religions no longer work for me. When I look at what is said and taught, much of it now seems to me, without the rosy glasses of need, to be very cruel. Who wants to believe in a being that acts in such an appalling way, even if it is self-sacrifice – why believe in the value of sacrificial killing at all? Why believe in a being who can be pushed, has to be pushed, by prayer and actions, to be benevolent and merciful? Life is tough enough without having to invent a being that needs to be cajoled into decent behaviour.

I cannot accept the beliefs that lie behind words like 'I am not worthy to receive…' as I know now that it is not constructive to so belittle myself. I would rather say: 'I have tried hard, and have not always succeeded in achieving my plans to behave kindly to others, but I have tried.' I cannot confess to and ask for forgiveness of some theoretical master of my behaviour, when I know that those of whom I should actually seek forgiveness for wrongs done are people, and it is to them that I should seek to do what I can to right the wrongs done.

I am aware that for many people the use of impersonal words, following traditional lines, is of value. Possibly such words help them face themselves, but often I suspect that they merely enable people to hide behind forms of words. Councils are being advised to avoid jargon. (I do not hold out much hope for this to happen because weak people like to increase their glory by grandiose verbiage and because plain speaking reveals the shallow emptiness of what is being said.) I would advise organised religions to avoid jargon too and then people might see that religious expressions (religious jargon), when unclothed, show a startling oddity of thought.

I am bored with having to demythologise words in services and religious texts all the time. For example: 'the devil tempting me' has to be interpreted into something like 'my own weakness or selfishness accounts for my actions.' Why not say that in the first place? 'The Kingdom come, God's will be done here on Earth'. Why not declare that we wish to aim to make the world a better, fairer, kinder place for all people?

I would like us to be able to gain from the moral, caring, thoughtful insights of many of the world's great religions, but without having to continue with (or trying to adapt) the baggage of old thoughts, formed in the pre-scientific, pre-psychological era. Of course we need to learn from ancient human wisdom but we must remain wide open to new discoveries and understanding, free to discard all that no longer holds true and is not consistent with the experiences of our twenty first century understanding.

I cannot slide back into the old comfort zone of the love of God who provided us with a saviour. I think we just have to live with whatever life throws at us as best we can, all the while being grateful for, and supportive and co-operative with, our fellow humans who have tried and are trying to make our separate journeys bearable. Kindness is the greatest virtue I now value.

Except – and here I recognise the effect of all that previous religious life of mine – I sometimes think that the universe shows some evidence of self-teaching. This particular Earth has changed from being just a hot and gaseous mess to a planet with sentient creatures and even a few self-aware, thinking creatures with incredible power to care for and to destroy it. Possibly many other planets have followed the same pathway. One day, perhaps, the universe will produce wise life forms which will be able, deliberately, to care for it. Does that mean that there is a long-term purpose in the system? Or some purpose-maker? I can accept that possibility, but in no way can I attach to this ultimate purpose-maker any of the notions now attached to God or gods.

Death is problematic to me still: the scientific certainty that death is the total end is not convincing enough. The world is never untouched by the fact that a particular person lived and died. While the living remember the dead, then they are still with us and, even when they are no longer remembered, the actions of the dead are still having an effect, like ripples in a pond. Physical death never is, cannot be, complete annihilation. Like Buddha, I can only ask: Who can know what happens after death? As I said, old ideas linger for me. But never the language – Don Cupitt might try hard to rehabilitate old words by redefining them – but then he is still trying to keep people in contact with the best of the past. For me it is all too late. However limited my thoughts may be, they are at least mine and I feel free, and I have one clear certainty: kindness is the greatest virtue.

Variations on a Given Theme

Anne Ashworth

1
The microscope has taught us to forget
The longsight lens, the larger mysteries.
It seems the astronomers have not spoken yet.

Specialists dance a blindfold minuet:
Minutes' minutiae, analyses.
The microscope has taught us to forget.

Vision reduces. Windows pose a threat.
Will double glazing put us at our ease?
It seems the astronomers have not spoken yet.

Division's multiplied, so why regret
The passing of addition, syntheses
The microscope has taught us to forget?

The telescopes will turn and pay their debt,
The giant scanners force us to our knees.
The microscope has taught us to forget,
But wait – the astronomers have not spoken yet.

2
We did consider the lilies
But still there is no vision.
Must the people perish?

Botanists fumble in fields,
Peering at pollen,
Skirting the crater where
The meteor's fallen.

Considering lilies, they forget
The astronomers have not spoken yet.
    We did consider the lilies.

Weathermen measure the wind,
Forecast a shower.
Botanists hurry indoors,
The lilies cower.
Considering clouds, weathermen fret.
The astronomers have not spoken yet
    And still there is no vision.

Astronomers close one eye
For concentration,
Circle the probing lens
In contemplation,
Considering if the stars will set.
The astronomers have not spoken yet.
    Must the people perish?

3
Spaces in space,
Time out of mind,
Somewhere the black holes lurk.
Who can erase
Sky writing signed
With such a question mark?

Question is truth.
Answers are always
False or fail to follow.
Respect the growth
Of silence, praise
The hint, the hole, the hollow.

The astronomers have not spoken yet.

The Elephant in the Garden

Kathleen McPhilemy

Yes; there is always the elephant;
the sky is the grey of his skin,
his legs are the crooked corners
that hold us, that pen us in.

I walk on the rain-soaked grass
carrying my new-born grandson;
he is settled by the flickering light,
but the droop of the rose reminds me
weeping its blood coloured petals
as they succumb to the blustering wind.

I have tried to find the New Eden
and ended up in shopping centres;
the meaning of garden is hidden
under plastic under glass under concrete.
I'm holding the light of the world
but he is innocence coded for conflict.
Cherubs and djinns glower over him
through the clouds of the 21st century.

We escape from the house to the garden
from our jarring clutter of words;
we seek in the garden for refuge
from the raging world outside.
But the elephant was there before us
the presence behind the rose,
the chill of this shadowy summer
his breathing beneath the breeze;
and the threat of his upraised foot
is the moment the sun goes in.

Scarlet Rose

On the death of my grand-daughter just before her birth

Sebastian Barker

Scarlet Rose, Scarlet Rose,
out of the darkness, look how she glows.

Fingers and forehead, her lips and her toes,
life in its origin, look how she grows.

'I am the child of the sun and the snows
made in the making all motherhood knows.

Reach out and touch me before I disclose
the rain in the wilderness where I repose.'

Scarlet Rose, Scarlet Rose,
look how she gravitates, look how she glows.

Scarlet Rose, Scarlet Rose,
gone in a moment, gone where she goes.

Scarlet Rose

Hilary Davies

Out in the marsh lies Scarlet Rose
Where the black Lea through its mudbanks
Past Old Ford and Three Mills and the Roman road flows.
Do you hear their feet flying? The tramp of men
Dying for empire again and again
Ever since we first cut down the alders with stone.

Out in the marsh lies Scarlet Rose:
The deer run on Epping hill and the beeches ring
With groves of blackbirds and the dun of hooves;
Look at the wild kites and model airplanes chasing
Their tails in the clouds! Look at the shroud
Of the dead queen in her hunting lodge
And the staircases of power.

Out in the marsh lies Scarlet Rose,
Who smiled in the darkness and never saw
Day or night. Cities, stand still.
Tyrants and governments, drop beneath the tides.
The Lea flows past their graveyards to the sea.

Out in the marsh where the salt wind blows,
Out in the marsh lies Scarlet Rose.

Interlocking Worlds

William Oxley

'Light and shade effects rivalling those of the greatest English poets' – V. NABOKOV

Noon shifts itself down Keats' Grove,
comes to rest under historic oaks, chestnuts
by South Hill Ponds. Sky peers
between floppy-haired trees, sees
its own cloud-gaze in motionless water.

A figure stands in rippling shade. Young
and nonchalant, his face catches
the passing glitter of up-struck light
from the pond's surface. Then watching
a fat mallard disturb its watery patch

he sees the sun's emissaries
dancing with delicious water nymphs,
feels he has looked right to the edge of things,
glimpsed imagination's interlocking worlds
that light and shade effects reveal –
feels he has witnessed oh-so-much.

In fact, he has seen poetry in action
                    and inaction:
grasped for a moment the meaning of light
that is the honey of being
and the shade that is its undoing.

The Substitute Sky

Lynne Wycherley

Each day we stare at screens,
a sly fluorescence, a not-quite sky
where swarms of data
aggregate and fly

while unseen cloud-and-sunlight
walks the grass, gold shoes
and grey, and beech and oak,
the green-leaved angels, pray.

Pilots of pixel storms,
what do we bring? Less talk,
less laughter, less sun on our skins;
our lives on hold, our children wired in.

Core addiction; captive eyes.
Outside the real world breathes, and dies.

Harm Done

Sylvia Moody

The damage that's done
may not be seen
or even felt.
But it is recorded.

Somewhere
in a dark place
a hand makes a note.
And in due time,
perhaps a lifetime later
top secret files are opened.

Eden Water

Christopher Truman

Eden, O our lost Eden!
a cry like starlight
at noon, ahead
for the trying.

It blurs in sharp rain
on a gantry walk,
l'abîme below, fangy
fish rounding a glow

of heaven above.
We stay the journey,
blister on rigging.
In the raw palm, a psalm.

Over summer months,
starlight a meal
for a parched rose,
sliced bitter apple

browning weal.
On a moonlit night,
bowl of pristine water
on the table, Eden!

patina of stardust.

The Streets of La Roue

Mimi Khalvati

1

From the red house on the fish quays
where the old harbour was, the plane trees
and the cobbles, in Wednesday drizzle
when thought travels on diagonals, colour
is pure and unlascivious, take the metro
from Sainte Catherine, via Jacques Brel
and Saint Guidon on the Erasmus Line
to Anderlecht – Anderlecht being, myth says,
a rough translation of 'the love of Erasmus' –
to find yourself between places, languages,
on the outer ring between city and countryside
where roads abruptly fade into fields, cows,
in a garden city whose streets commemorate
the aspirations of its founders and its people.

2

La Roue is on the outer ring. La Roue
could have been a blacksmith's wheel,
La Roue could have been a torturer's wheel:
spin it – *roue, roue, roue,* in a backstreet,
a hoop and a stick and here come the twenties,
a little bruiser in his grey shorts, grey shirt.
Here come the pavements, double crocodile
of nuns with their charges, the tramlines, river,
the lake where the children bathed. Here
come the houses, big ones, little ones, four
small wooden ones in a block that in fire
would burn. Here come the Belgian, French,
the Spanish and Portuguese and here come
the old who were born and still live here.

3
Like an old film star, the lone magnolia
is in flower but this is not Sunset Boulevard,
this is *Droits de l'Homme*, boasting mailboxes
in metal, wood, tin, most like birdhouses
with two tiny dormer windows looking out,
perplexed. Where is the postman? Where
are the addressees? *Attention au Chien!
C'est moi qui monte la garde ici!* But
what does he guard? The cherub urns,
barbecues, slides and trikes, basketball posts,
looking up and barking, the number plaques?
What need for number when each doorway
is marked by its own carefully chosen tree-tile,
wall bracket, weathervane, carriage lamp?

4
On *Rue de l'Émancipation*, parked in a white van,
Façade Express undertakes the cleaning of facades.
But nothing is what it seems. Under the asphalt
run the old tramlines, under the tramlines, damned
for all its sewage to run eternally underground,
what might have been a tourists' café-side river.
But for all the builders' rubble, plastic bags,
piping, wires, concrete blocks, tiling, planks
and paving stones, there are giant Brussels sprouts
vying with camellias, geraniums and compost
sitting beside the pebbledash, japonica flowering,
rhododendron and broom and in a window,
behind the yellow primulas, a black and white cat,
black-nosed with a soot mark, looking anxious.

5
From No. 4, particularly pretty with an espaliered
tree and a climbing rose on a three-pole arch,
the sound of running water, a windchime
and an awning still bearing traces of artificial
Christmas snow, a lady opens her window to ask:
Vous cherchez quelqu'un? I am looking
for La Roue, I am looking for its guiding spirit,
where will I find it, *chez vous, chez vous,
chez eux?* Look, here is a bench for poets
and the elderly, a crescent where daisies grow
freely on the verge, *Place Ernest S'Jonghers*
overlooked by an orange crane and tremendous
sudden drumming from some den or loft
where a teenager drives them all berserk.

6
But let us praise folly, for 'He who loves
vehemently no longer lives in himself
but in what he loves…', Erasmus says,
and no more so than on *Rue du Symbole,*
where a young girl in a tracksuit is pulling
on a pink string a toddler on a trike, sucking
a dummy, surveying the world; a grandma
in a long brown robe and hejab accompanies
a gaggle of Moroccan school kids; an old spruce
wears a wild afro of ivy, a baby stone rabbit
nibbles at weeds and on net curtains, embroidered,
spreads an idyll of ponies, pastures, windmills
and turtledoves flying out of their cages to flirt.

7
'… and his joy is in proportion to his withdrawal
from self and his preoccupation with what is
outside himself' our guiding spirit, for I believe
Erasmus himself has been invoked, continues:
'When the soul meditates on travelling without
this use of its limbs, this is certainly insanity.'
And suddenly Soul arrives at a basketball ground
and, not wishing to travel unfingered, unlimbed,
straddles a bench to carve a soulful message:
pour la vie mon bb, invoking the names
of Christel, Souliman, Ismael. Soul kicks
at broken sidelight glass, plastic fork tines
scattered in the dust of *Place Ministre Wauters*
and asks: 'Who once ate here under the elms?'

8
On the corner of *Rue de l'Énergie*,
you will find the boulangerie/fromagerie
of Tonton Garby. In a French beret
and moustache, Monsieur Tonton
(whose less energetic brother serves
alternate days in a seven-day week)
holds forth in English, in French.
He has lived here for 43 years,
travelled all over – Oxford Street,
Piccadilly Circus, America (here
he bursts into an American accent)
and once, with his family, to Sri Lanka.
'Come on,' he cried, 'let's do the elephant tour!
Everything, everything!' And so they did.

9
'The more perfect the love, the greater
the madness,' Erasmus concludes in his praise
of folly. And folly it is, surely, to come upon
an open space in the *Rue des Colombophiles*
where, beyond a fence of corrugated iron strips,
car panels, wire fencing, is a flat area of allotments,
well dug but empty of produce save for a few
yellow potato flowers and some far greenery.
Back gardens flaunt chickens and daffodils,
a fine cedar fronting a row of poplars, the chimneys
of the concrete factory, the railway bridge, trains
going to Ghent and, over the fence at the bottom end
of the allotments, helmeted cyclists gliding past
on the canalside like ducks in a shooting gallery.

10
Doves cooing on the *Rue des Huit Heures*
bring you to the *Plaine des Loisirs*. Pleasure,
more folly. Sun sets above the black plane trees
and on a bench this time, *ALO MAMAN*,
Je t'aime Valentin, are messages from Kelly.
A young one in her mother's arms, stretching out
a baby arm, is calling repeatedly like the dove,
'da-ddy, da-ddy'. Grass is littered with daisies
and the long thin diagonal shadows of the trees
underline the white lines the daisies seem to follow
like shadow-writing. A blade of a boy in a black suit
with a black dog yanks on the lead, making the dog
snarl and twist and half-leap as if on circus training.
The glittering of the grass swells like waves at sea.

11
We've come full circle back to *Place de la Roue*
but this time behind the church, once too small,
now, rebuilt, too big. After all, it's only a moderate
garden city, swelling with immigrants' kids:
these two girls, one with bad eyesight and glasses,
both with long brown ringlets, bright blue rollerblades,
legs splayed like young deer finding their legs,
this tubby boy, pushing his sister, *Vite, vite!*
Two boys bending to their mothers' headscarved
brows with kisses. And the young Moslem women,
laughing, handling the baby in the pram as lightly,
with as little concern as their mothers before them did.
This little girl in plum, standing a foot away, swinging
her arms violently from side to side like a windmill.

12
'A glutton for letters,' Erasmus said of himself,
his humanism trying to unite, above the confusion
of beliefs and races, all the clerics who desired
not to betray the cause of the spirit. In his house
lie a cast of his cranium, fragments of his coffin.
In the Room of Rhetoric, a statue of him stands,
the saint holding back his torn entrails, carrying
carpenter's tools and hoe, square and compass.
In profile, sharpened quill in hand, studied hands
on an open book, fingers ringed, he sits writing.
He wears three coats, so cold were the winters,
and the black hat from which he was never parted.
Outside, leaf ponds float his adages – UBI BENE,
IBI PATRIA, brass letters half-submerged, rusting.

The End of the Canticle

John of the Cross

Bride to Bridegroom:
Let us be happy, my love.
In your beauty let us go together
to the woods and up the mountain
where the pure waters run.
Into the thicket now let us go further.

Then we shall keep climbing
higher to the deep stone caverns
which are well hidden.
We will go in
and there we'll taste the pomegranate wine.

There you could show me
everything my soul has ever craved.
Then you could give me,
since you are life to me,
what you promised me the other day.

The breathing of the breezes,
the singing of the nightingale most sweet,
the grove of graceful trees
in the gentle night,
the flame that's burning but which does not hurt.

Nobody was looking.
Neither did Aminadab appear,
and all around us rested,
and the men on horses
rode on downhill within sight of water.

The Walking Heart

Sebastian Barker

The road to the miraculous meanders
through the living forest to the water
fallen from the sky and the high mountains.
The fat river slides under the low bridges,
swollen with the miracle of rain.
Silver fishes sparkle in the sun
seen by an elder's eye on the long walk home.
Brighter than the greenery of paint,
the rain-intoxicated trees and moss
and grass and grove and glade and field, sing
out of the love on fire in the walking heart.

Oldies Abroad in Spring

Adele Davide

The sun's come
first day
not yet a wild swinging hope
in this other land of wildflowers.
Windflowers white
and lilac.
Daisies. Yellow unknowns.
Adders hiding in long grass.
Foxes stalking.
Spring used to be an excitement
of imagined futures
of all the glorious happenstance
of men.
Today we walk slow
afraid to break a hip
ecstatic we can move at all.

Maytime

Dinah Livingstone

He and she walked out into a May meadow
and made love under a flowering tree.
The sun lit the buttercups
among the new green grass
and shone on the shape of each fresh leaf
pushed out by a rush of juice.
A bird chorus described the sweetness
up to the soft surrounding blue.
The ground was damp and smelt of home.

My beloved is agile and strong
and delicate as a leaping deer.
Come to me. Come.
Then in bliss they rested.

She cupped in her hand
what was now as little and sticky
as a just hatched chick.
Uccellino, he told her and smiled
irresistibly. She kissed him.
After a while: *Eppur si muove* –
it does move – he said.

Happy, they laughed
and – honouring great Galileo
who fought for the truth
about what our Earth is and does,
against false religion,
and cocked a snook
at the priests in black gowns
who condemned him –
they made love again.

Peter Bellinger Brodie

1815-1897: Rector and geologist

Daphne Rock

I imagine him in an old felt hat, booted and caped,
wet with dawn mist as he tapped out
an insect from long solitude in the Blue Lias:
the first man to set eyes on so beautiful a thing,
evidence of evolution tucked in his cassock.

Bible at hand and
in the spare moments between sermons
he studied evidence of Warwick under ice,
under deep seas and spattered with volcanoes.

Keen clerics everywhere
roamed rocks and chasms, stood tip toe on cliffs
down which might tumble Genesis:
the heavens and earth and all the host of them.

Peter Bellinger Brodie, clerk in holy orders,
a man of God with science in his trust.
His **History of Fossil Insects** stayed
this side of heresy – safely, when he died
they said *he loved God's world.*

At the Grave of Herbert Spencer

Highgate Cemetery, London

Tom Rubens

The small marble sepulchre reads
That here his ashes are contained.
One feels that these are now
All he would have wanted to be
Identified as, given his
Ceaseless, unflagging involvement
With the tangible and observable.
His being one day only cinders
Would surely have given no offence,
Had it been suggested to him
      as his future state;
On the contrary, one can picture his
Delighting at the thought's precision,
And at its not in any way
Invalidating what he had to say
      about life.

The individual, he showed us,
Is a single day in evolutionary time,
Though one that can attain its
Noontide and pulsating zenith;
Human plasm is the subject of
The planet's venture in creation,
And we its passing episodes.
He taught us to take our transience
In good part, and to be concerned for
The far future, when even the
Rarest animal beauty and gifts

This Life on Earth

Known to us might be surpassed;
And if they were, their superseders too
Would also one day be residue,
A reduction to minimal substance,
Placed beneath inscriptions which
Further-still humanity would absorb.

Overhead, the wind drives clouds
Across the blue, and now and then
A shadow shows on the stone smoothness.
Lives pass, all passes, one thinks.
The tightening in the stomach which
This thought brings lasts only
        a moment,
Relieved and dispelled by
The compactness of the marble shape,
Its modest ornamentation and
The decisive cut of the letters.
One realises he would not have wished
For any excess; just the solid, the
Adequate and firm. Which one resolves
To be, in bearing his discoveries,
His demanding and toughening truths
About the grandeur of the whole.

End of Book

Anne Beresford

While we're waiting
let's open the champagne
and remember summer is not over yet.

This time of evening
makes me sad
and I long for home.

How still it is
but the fisherman's wife
said the sea was 'choppy' out there from the shore.

Let's not waste these last hours
talking of our past
or speculating on imaginary futures.

We're together, I hear your breath,
hold me close,
leave the final sentence to the Earth.

A Chronicle of the Ages of Life on a Small Planet

Dominic Kirkham

This life on Earth is a strange thing. It is but an infinitesimally small part of something much greater – a Cosmos: not just a 'thing', or even 'every thing', but a dynamic whole. Life is its expression. Life embraces everything that is. It has no past, no future, no boundaries nor limits, just 'everything'. In its vast embrace everything is simply present.

This Earth is a fragment, a 'specimen', within a vast cosmic incubator of life that is constantly bringing all things into being. Its structure is of scarcely imaginable physical forces whose energy has the ability to generate mass. Not just formless abstraction but shape. Even the vast amorphous nebulae are shaped mathematical structures; so chaos gives rise to unlimited possibilities. And therein lies the secret of life: a self-generating system of energy, which is self-organising, expressing itself in endless forms most beautiful. This Earth is simply an expression and a part of this awesome process of creativity.

But just let me stop you there! How can I know this? Because of something even more amazing, perhaps unique to this life on Earth: consciousness. Yes, life on Earth, in all its thrusting and thriving diversity has produced creatures with awareness. Through this possibility one creature brought forth knowledge. In the story of the universe it was a unique moment: life now had the capacity to know itself. On this Earth – a small insignificant planet, but viewed from space truly a star – there was now consciousness of the cosmic story.

In its genesis knowledge reflected not just on this life but the very nature of its origin. Brought forth by chemical interactions, whose discharge shimmers across the surface of the brain, knowledge replicates the gossamer membrane of life that envelopes the corporeal surface of this Earth. The human brain seems poised as a vital point of equilibrium between the infinitesimally small, sub-atomic world, and the infinitely large structures of interstellar space. In the line of density which stretches from atomic structures to galactic masses the human stands at exactly the mid-point, ideally placed to observe their story.

And what a story! This life on Earth arose from vital cosmic fragments, gathered together and over a vast period of three billion years moulded into unique microbial forms. The Earth became a workshop for life. The nucleic structures that underpin all life forms on this Earth were gradually put in place. The self-organising capacity of matter – drawing energy from the environment to create delicately balanced states of equilibrium – enabled ever more complex molecules to aggregate. The biochemical processes of replication created a fractal beauty, which would henceforth be the signature of all life within the Earth's newly created biosphere.

A living tissue began to clothe this Earth, the web of life. Vital processes were developed such as replication, metabolism and photosynthesis, which enabled life to absorb energy and expand. All the key processes of life were first worked out on a microbial level, which indeed still accounts for 98% of the life forms of this life on Earth. So secretive was the work that all the great kingdoms of life lay hidden from view, so much so that at one point it was even called the 'azoic era' – the era without life.

How mistaken this was! Hidden from view, life had prepared all its tools ready for a magnificent burgeoning forth, an epiphany of its hitherto secret mysteries. Then, 500 million years ago, the multi-cellular forms of life began to appear; all the thirty-five great phyla of the animal kingdom suddenly emerged, almost in the twinkling of an eye. Indeed, the eye itself appeared and species began to look upon this life on Earth for the first time. This life on Earth had crossed a vital threshold into the luminescent life of day. The phanerozoic (or visible) era of life had dawned.

This life on Earth now began to express itself in ever greater, ever more diverse forms, exploding across the Earth like a great pyrotechnic display of species. Every possible niche, every livable space was now colonised by some life form. Every creature strove to increase in size until they achieved their optimal existence. Their structural range poised daringly between the microcosm of the molecules and the macrocosm of the stars: it was the mesocosm – the realm of the multicellular creatures.

But then, as the story seemed to reach a dizzying apogee of biodiversity, there came forth the creature with knowledge. It was to be a particularly fateful – if not fatal – moment for this life on Earth. At first this creature was overwhelmed and awestruck by the incomprehensible majesty of life of which it was part. So much so that humans – for that is what they were, creatures formed from the earth, humus – not only venerated but worshipped nature; they thought of themselves in terms of the animals, who seemed so much more powerful and splendid. They even built temples to worship them.

Then things changed. Humans, clever humans, began to manipulate life for their own ends, reordering the Earth for their own benefit and in accordance with their dreams. Typically, the oldest and greatest structures ever built by them were erected for no earthly natural need, but so that their owners could enjoy eternal life amongst the stars. Nature was not enough; they wanted more – always more: a super-nature. This would be the pattern for the future: with their minds on the heavens and feet on the Earth, the world was there simply to be trampled on, whilst journeying to greater dreams.

It was to be the beginning of the end! Other creatures learnt to fear them. Those that didn't were the first to be exterminated. Becoming evermore numerous, evermore inventive, evermore powerful, humans became the lords of this Earth. They assumed the view that all life was theirs, to do with as they liked, until a point was reached – at the end of the twentieth century of their time – when another decisive threshold in the history of this life on Earth was crossed. Not only did humans then consume more than the Earth could produce, but in consuming they destroyed the very sources of life on Earth.

As with the crossing of previous vital thresholds in the story of this life on Earth, a new name was given to the new era. It was the eremozoic: the era of solitude. The statistics were frightening: 12% of the world's birds, 21% of its mammals, 30% of its amphibians, 31% of its reptiles, 37% of its fishes, 70% of its plant species… became threatened with extinction. But it was not just the scale but the speed at which this happened. In just a few decades the achievement of millions of years of evolution was wiped out.

The rapidity in which this human-induced holocaust consumed the life of Earth was unprecedented in its entire history. 100 species a day became extinct at the beginning of the twenty-first century. For the first time in the history of this life on Earth, one species had taken on the power of a geological force that was wholly destructive. Though claiming unique intelligence, in fact they achieved unique folly: no other creature had ever destroyed its own means of survival, as well as that of all others. Little would remain of life on Earth except one species amidst a scene of utter desolation.

It was at that time the Vice-President of the then most environmentally destructive nation on Earth startled humans by promoting an inconvenient truth: civilisation was killing the Earth. The forests felled; the Earth torn open; the skies emptied of birds; almost incomprehensibly, the seas were emptied of fish. The bee-loud glades were silenced and song birds heard no more over the land. An era of solitude indeed; but that was only the lesser part of it. Through their fuel driven technologies the very air the humans breathed began to be poisoned, the climate heated and the seas acidified. Not only were they driving all the great species of animals to extinction, they were destroying their entire habitat. Life on Earth was now becoming unsustainable.

Nothing like this had ever happened to life on Earth since the Permian crisis of life 250 million years previously. At that time similar effects (from geological causes) of the heating of the land and acidification of the seas led to the disappearance of 95% of life forms on Earth. Fortunately, Earth showed its amazing powers of recovery, regaining that homeostasis or dynamic equilibrium, which was at the very core of all life processes. Even though the self-correcting nature of this life on Earth was one of its most subtle features, it took some twenty million years before the damage was repaired and new ecosystems created. What made the crisis in the eremozoic era more grievous was the incomparable richness and diversity that the flora and fauna had now achieved.

As with all plagues, having reached a crescendo of destructiveness, in the end the *'disseminate primatemaia'* (plague of people) ebbed away. It took less than a century. By the middle of the twenty-first century, millions of people had been displaced from their homes, partly from the rising sea levels resulting from the melting of the great polar ice caps, but also from the shortage of drinking water. Shortage of energy made life unsustainable in a megalopolis, the vast conurbations where most of the population lived. Shortage of food caused riots and the critical shortage of all resources led to global instability and war, fanned by extreme ideologies and irrational beliefs.

It was an apocalyptic age. Nothing like this had been seen before in human history, though there had been intimations, as when the Roman Empire collapsed, after a super-volcanic eruption in southern Asia disrupted the global climate, or as with several early civilisations in central and south America, which collapsed in the wake of environmental depredation and climate change. In the great European conflict of the seventeenth century, which coincided with a deterioration of the climate, the population of that continent plummeted by over one third and civil society almost collapsed. The same now happened again, but on a global scale. Small groups of humans clung on to life in miserable circumstances, reverting to the savagery that had never been far beneath the surface of their civilised life, even in the good times.

Not only knowledge but essential survival skills were lost. Having become largely urban, most humans had already lost all knowledge of the land and the skills to work with nature; obsessed by their technologies, they had become ignorant of the life of the Earth on which they lived. Indeed, this deracination was the source of their problems. So, in a desiccated landscape with ever increasing temperatures they gradually disappeared. The final *coup de grâce* came when the super-volcano beneath 'old faithful' in Yellowstone Park erupted in one of its cyclical cataclysms – proving, once more, true to its name! Thus humans joined the 99% of species which over the aeons this life on Earth in all its fecundity had created, only to be set aside as other life forms replaced them.

As always, this life on Earth continued. The cause of the planetary perturbation was corrected and the cleansing power of extinction allowed the ever creative power of life on Earth to bring forth new forms, marvellously adapted to new circumstances. So a new age dawned. It could be called the ecozoic, when life regained the equilibrium of its natural rhythms, but perhaps more appropriate is the name cryptozoic, or hidden age, for it was destined to be forever unrecorded. Though these events could still be observed – due to the time consumed by the speed of light – from the most distant galaxies of the universe, like Haufen, Coma and Hercules, long after they had taken place here on Earth.

The relics of previous ages became fossils, reminders of another phase in the timeline of life. These now included not only the remains of creatures but also of their creations: technical artifices, monumental machines, inscribed remains of plans for a brave new world, even bizarre religious texts, which revealed an ultimate hubris – that this life on Earth was not enough: that a species wanted an after-life, even eternal life. Such fossils became the tombstones of these conquistadors of consumption, who in wanting everything lost everything. Their epitaph could be, and was, summarised in one word: greed.

This chronicle has no further knowledge of that or subsequent eras, only that when these events took place, this life on Earth had barely run for half its course. This life on Earth now continued, freed from the threat of an insatiable destructive greed. But finally an even greater threat appeared. The energy that had powered this life on Earth had come not just from within itself, from its biochemical processes, but from far beyond. It had come from Earth's solar partner, for so long a largely benign but occasionally threatening partner. Now, as this partner aged, it became ever more irascible and difficult to live with. As is the way with stars, it began to expand into a red giant and consumed the Earth. This life on Earth finally ended, an event of such insignificance in the vast emporium of the universe that it went unnoticed and unrecorded.

But this narrative was written to show that it was not entirely without appreciation. This life on Earth was a wonderful and unparalleled achievement. Yet the narrative of its achievement is full of ironies. It is a product of that consciousness which this life on Earth had made possible, yet the very point in time when consciousness became aware of the true nature of the global web of life was the point at which it was destroyed; the creature of knowledge, which had so prided itself on its sapiental abilities, remained like all other creatures so driven by the instincts of reproduction and predation that these became its destruction; its dreams for the future and preoccupations with the past became so prevalent that it became almost entirely distracted from the present – it mistook its fantasies for reality.

The reality was that this life on Earth was only ever a small part of the life of the universe which enveloped it. That remains. Life. It has no purpose or destiny, only its ever creative expression. It simply is, a presence – its own epiphany. Its rhythms are eternal: ebb and flow, light and dark, systole and diastole, waxing and waning. All is simply life, simple and unique, but above all, beautiful. Every genus or species reflects but a part of its kaleidoscope – like the prismatic raindrop, which breaks open the rainbow in the summer storm, or frost which gleams on the Earth with a diaphanous sparkle on a winter's day, or the smallest flower, which clothes itself in golden petals. All reflect but a facet – marvel at it. Consider the lilies of the field, consider the birds in the air, listen to their song, consider the setting sun clothed in its cauldron of clouds. Here is a magic the mind can scarcely comprehend. Consider this life whilst one can. There is no other.

This Life in the Physical World

A Scientist's Testimony

Helen Bellamy

This account focuses solely on those parts of her life when the author has been engaged in a struggle to understand how science relates to life in the physical world. It leaves undescribed her efforts to make sense of religion and how that relates to life on Earth. Suffice it to say that the two investigations have run very much in parallel.

Because the rain was coming down in torrents, there was nothing else to be done but wait in the college entrance until it became practicable to emerge. Whilst standing there I reflected on the seminar I'd just attended. It was early in 1966 and that great scientist Herman Bondi, just returned from the States, had explained to us the new theory being propounded there by Murray Gell-Mann.[26] That theory, published in 1967, resulted in the 1969 award to Gell-Mann of the Nobel prize for physics. It proposed that all sub-atomic particles are combinations of truly elementary but never-to-be-seen particles called quarks.

The theory was exciting and its mathematics extremely elegant. It fitted all known sub-atomic particles into a single framework, the empty positions in that framework suggesting where new particles (since detected) would be available for discovery. My worry was this: Gell-Mann confidently predicted the existence of supposedly unobservable quarks on the sole basis that their presence would make for attractive mathematics. Why, I asked

---

26 http://nobelprize.org/nobel_prizes/physics/laureates/1969/gell-mann-bio.html

myself, should mathematical simplicity be a reliable indicator of truth?

It was not only the proposed existence of quarks that caused me to worry about the relationship between mathematics and physical reality. My recent studies had shown me that not only the entities physicists used in their work (for example, forces) but whole theories containing them (like Newtonian mechanics), long assumed valid because of their mathematical coherence and beauty as well as their practical success, had been shown to conflict with observation. These theories were now declared 'approximately true', a description I felt about as helpful as 'approximately pregnant': it indicated ignorance rather than certainty or truth.

In what sense, I wondered, was science true? Clearly theories must be in line with the outcomes of observation. All that such conformity guarantees, however, is that in certain significant respects the theories successfully convey truth about the world. They are like stories set in the world – fictions with a basis in reality – and familiarity with them gives us some understanding of – and so control over – the world around us. But when a favourite story turns out to be misleading (perhaps it had us believing in fairies), whilst we might continue make use of it, a new story is needed (replacing the fairies with our parents, maybe) that takes account of our new knowledge. When Rutherford's well-supported account of the structure of the atom proved inconsistent with Newton's mechanics, a new story about sub-atomic particles was needed and this was provided by quantum theory. Quarks might really exist or else be fictional, but whichever, the story about them helps small-particle physicists with their work of making sense of the world.

A similar way of answering my question about the truth of science was to regard it as a set of tools with which to get a grip on the world. When, for example, Copernicus moved away from an Earth-centred universe, he was not motivated by the search for truth but for a means of making tractable calculations of the positions of heavenly bodies. He made no claim that the sun was in reality at the centre of the universe. He simply pointed out that working on that basis made the sums involved very much more straightforward. In practice we all are happy to reach for whichever view is more useful in the context of the minute – we talk in geocentric terms of sunset and in a heliocentric way about the third rock.

The conclusions I reached at this period of my life were the assumptions that underpinned many later years of teaching mathematical physics. My most astute students would identify some bewildering dissimilarity between my approach and that of their physics teacher – who took science to be the direct truth about the world – when he covered the same material. It was fun to ask them questions that helped them to identify the difference between our two understandings of science.

*

Back in the spring of 1968, I spent much of my time in an office at the top of a tower block in Cardiff, covering sheet after sheet of paper with mathematics and then consigning each one to the waste paper bin. I'd been fascinated by quantum mechanics (QM) and had decided to spend a year pursuing my interest. QM had shattered any notion I might otherwise have managed to retain that the world was deterministic – that it was regulated by simple linkages between cause and effect. At the sub-atomic level an event may have several potential outcomes and which one will occur is something we cannot predict. We can only know in advance the relative probabilities of the various possible outcomes. Even more disconcertingly, in some cases the outcome (whether, for instance, electrons behave like waves or like particles) can turn out to depend on how we choose to observe it (watching the arrival of the electrons at a screen or registering them as they pass). Newton, Galileo and many since had seen the divine mind ordering the world by means of deterministic laws of nature. Now it is clear that, fundamentally, the physical world is a law unto itself, except in so far as human involvement shapes it. (As in Darwin's evolutionary theory, so in physics: we cannot think of ourselves in isolation from the world of which we are part.)

Sitting at the top of my tower in Cardiff, I was working through, time after time, a paper on electron states in an impure solid. 'You'll find something in that,' was the only advice from my supervisor. Week after week I searched for 'something' and at last – what relief! – found it: an error in the mathematics. I checked and rechecked – definitely an error – and then began to work out its consequences for the rest of the paper's argument. The revised mathematics was no less complicated, but showed a pattern hitherto absent. In triumph I reported this progress to my supervisor. 'Good,' he said, 'now go and work out what that means.'

At this point my working day changed: in alternate sessions I wrote up what I'd done so far and then spent time thinking about what it might mean. As I thought, I doodled, and so the waste paper basket continued to be full at the end of each day. My writing was coming along well but the thinking was getting me nowhere – until suddenly I realised that the doodling was becoming more purposeful. I focused on my drawing and before long had produced a series of small diagrams. Each was made up of a straight line and several loops and represented a single term in my mathematics. Before long I could replace my horribly complex equations by a series of simple diagrams. My supervisor was delighted and the QM enthusiasts, to whom we presented my diagram system at a conference, were impressed. I myself, though, was just bewildered about what exactly I had achieved – and I remained so for more than thirty-five years!

*

Retirement presented me with the opportunity to seek greater understanding of the nature of science. I had three major concerns. One pressing question was how it is that science undergoes revolutions, suddenly adopting a new theory whilst continuing to make use of the old one, now known to be false. Aeroplanes and bridges are still designed using Newtonian mechanics, a theory discredited a hundred or so years ago. I was still worrying about those quarks and about whether entities in mathematical physics are mental or physical phenomena. Finally, I had still no clear understanding of the way in which the world can be represented by formulae and pictures: I was still bemused by my diagram system. All these puzzles had been set aside whilst I'd been raising a family and undertaking caring responsibilities alongside earning a living. Now I was able to give them attention.

I found that during the decades when I'd had other things to think about, work had been going on that established a whole body of ideas about the nature of scientific theory and its application. Following the publication in the 1960s of Kuhn's famous book *The Structure of Scientific Revolutions*[27] (that introduced the notion of a 'paradigm shift'), philosophical thinking about science had grown until it now forms a distinct discipline in several universities in the UK and the US. The questions that I had neglected for so long had become the focus of intense academic attention.

In the 60s, when I had first struggled to understand what I was doing when involved in mathematical physics, the dominant approach was hypothetico-deductive. The physical world was assumed to exemplify the rules of logic and so from a hypothesis firmly supported by experimental evidence other truths about the world could be deduced. By identifying new mathematical relationships that were well verified by observation and combining these with already known laws, new truths could be established by the mathematical physicist. These were passed on to his[28] laboratory colleagues for experimental confirmation. Truth in physics was understood to involve correspondence

---

27 http://www.des.emory.edu/mfp/Kuhn.html
28 Women physicists were very few and far between at this time: I'd guess between 2% and 5% of the profession.

between mathematics and reality and also coherence between one theory and another. It was these unspoken but all-pervasive realist assumptions – still made today by perhaps the majority of physicists – which had made conflicting theories, quarks and scientific representation so difficult for me to comprehend.

Now a whole range of views was available for my consideration, along with arguments for and against them. I was satisfied to find the realist position very effectively undermined by a whole series of arguments, for instance that from underdetermination: there are as many theories as you like that will fit a given set of observations, so how are we to know which one is true? The most powerful argument against scientific realism, though, follows from the recognition of revolutions in the history of science. For the realist, when a new theory suddenly supersedes an established one, what had up to now been true has to be acknowledged to be false! For the scientific anti-realist,[29] the new theory is just a new tool that can be used to manipulate areas of experience that the old theory had been shown not to fit. The old theory should not be abandoned, but its use restricted to those parts of the physical world in which it adequately fits the observational data. There is no need to call on relativity theory when setting up an aeroplane route – Newtonian mechanics serves well for that purpose – but we certainly must use relativity in our calculations if we are planning a trip through space.

*

It is extremely difficult to be realist about scientific theories; to hold that they tell us the truth about reality leads to all sorts of contradictions. Now, theories propose how scientific entities are related. If theories do not fully match reality, what part of them is fictional? Is it the entities, or the structural relations between

---

29 SOF aficionados may be surprised by this usage. In science, 'non-realism' is the title of one very specific viewpoint proposed by Arthur Fine.

them, or both? The person whose answer to this question most satisfies me is the Princeton professor Bas van Fraassen.

Van Fraassen long since adopted studied agnosticism about the reality of the unobservable entities, like quarks, whose existence is suggested by mathematical physics. He is only prepared to claim as certainly existing what is publicly and directly observable. We can agree, he would say, that the tree which each of us observes each time we cross the quad really exists. We cannot be certain about the reality of any of the sub-atomic particles that we are unable to see with the naked eye. The existence of some of these particles – electrons for example – is highly likely, but not certain. Yes, we can see an electron beam illuminating a cathode ray tube, but what we see is a flash on a screen, not an electron. We may measure an electric current, which we believe to be a stream of electrons, but what we actually observe is a pointer on a dial.

Van Fraassen's critics include not only realists, who insist that whatever entities the mathematics suggests to us must exist, and complete sceptics, who refute the existence of the tree in the quad. Other anti-realists[30] include entity-only realists like Ian Hacking,[31] who holds that whatever we can manipulate must be real (so electrons are real because we can spray them around a cathode ray tube) and structural realists, like Steven French,[32] who propose that the entities themselves are not real, but the relations between them are. (No, I can't get my head round that either!)

When published, van Fraassen's view was the subject of much criticism, centring on what was and was not directly observable. He dealt effectively with the various undermining examples proposed, to create a firm boundary. The moons of Saturn are directly observable – or would be if we got ourselves near enough to them. Microscopic phenomena are not observable – we shall

---

30 http://www.princeton.edu/~fraassen/cv/index.htm
31 http://en.wikipedia.org/wiki/Ian_Hacking
32 http://www.philosophy.leeds.ac.uk/Staff/SF/Index.htm

never see them with the naked eye. Unicorns are observable – or would be if they existed. Rainbows, although they exist and can be seen, count as unobservable because different observers will disagree about their position; and mental delusions are not observable because they are not publicly available at all. I can see the sense in all of this, and am happy to be agnostic about the existence of quarks.

*

'Constructive empiricism' is the title van Fraassen gives to his understanding of science. He sets himself firmly in the empiricist tradition that regards knowledge as a set of instruments with which we attempt to gain control over the world. He sees science as humanly constructed, with the interpretation of experience taking priority over reasoning. I find his views interesting and his arguments compelling.

I hope to devote some of the coming summer to studying his latest book *Scientific Representation*. Already I understand that scientific representation can be thought of as semantic rather than syntactical, pictorial rather than analytical. The model that depicts the world may be artistic, mathematical or metaphorical and any logic we apply will refer to the model rather than the world it represents.

In constructing a model, certain features of the physical world are selected to be depicted in a particular form, on a particular scale and from a particular point of view. Consider, by way of example, the London tube map that represents underground lines – allocating to each a colour – and tube stations, and symbols signifying the presence of adjacent main line stations. Only these features of the network are modelled. If the map is to be of use to you, you must know where you are, as well as where you want to go. The map is of no help in estimating the time your journey may take or your direction of travel. Similarly, a scientific model selects features of the world and shows how these are related. Any such model's usefulness is limited: QM will no more help you to design a car engine than a tube map will help you to cross central London on foot.

I now understand that my 1968 diagrams in fact represent an 'electron's-eye' view of a journey through an impure solid, showing encounters with various nuclei of atoms along the way. They give no indication, though, of such factors as the electron's speed or its direction of travel.

*

I spent much time during the summer of 2007 working in or beside my motor caravan in the countryside. I was reading and writing about van Fraassen's 2002 book *The Empirical Stance* and the reactions – several of horror! – that it provoked. The volume consisted of his Terry Lectures given at Yale – on religion in the light of science and philosophy – a series whose previous presenters had included such well known thinkers as Paul Tillich, Paul Ricoeur, Hans Küng, Erich Fromm and Carl Gustav Jung.

In this book van Fraassen suggests that *belief* in a scientific theory, in the sense of acceptance of its factuality, is completely inappropriate. Instead he advocates that a well-supported theory be *accepted as empirically adequate*, that is, in line with observation. He proposes that a scientist who is working within a particular theoretic tradition must adopt a *stance,* involving both where and how he stands with respect to his theory. The position he takes up is acceptance of the empirical adequacy of his theory. The attitude he adopts will include *commitment* to his theory, involving an emotional attachment. (It was that invoking of *emotion* in this explanation of the scientific project that caused the shocked response from other philosophers of science.)

I find this idea of stance – as commitment to (as opposed to belief in) an empirically adequate model or story – very helpful. I should love one day to have moved far enough ahead in my thinking to be able to write under the heading *The Religious Stance*.

My Life and Colourful Times

Anna Sutcliffe

I recently suffered a bad retinal bleed and lost the remains of my centre vision. This is a bad thing for an artist. A friend, an eye-consultant, rang: 'Can you see colour?' The thought of not seeing colour was so dreadful, I felt elated. As a child I loved green. It was not *primus inter pares*, it was qualitatively different.

'What's your favourite colour, love?' the adults would say.

'Green'.

And they would chortle as if they'd put in a coin and got chocolate.

All special women should wear green. I knew that brides wore white (until the war, when they wore stern suits, Cuban heels and carried vast round bouquets of carnations) but in that they were misguided. I used to paint brides' dresses in magazines with a paintbox colour called green bice. Who am I to quarrel with George Herbert? Green has often been the colour of life and resurrection. All the same, try Vermilion. This is my haiku:

> Vermilion boots
> crinkle the colour of life
> over frail ankles.

I used to buy Vermilion velvet. That was for stage costumes. I was heavily into theatre in education (think 1960s, 1970s). Now, imagine this scenario: The little boy furrows the velvet between his fingers. The light on the ridges is peach colour. He strokes the nap with a flat palm. I say the word: 'Vermilion'. As a pigment it is cinnabar (chemically that is mercuric sulphide), the word has something to do with worms, the colour is subtle – not orange, not scarlet.

I made a hanging called *Ripe and Unripe Verges*. The sky is not red, neither is the grass. Teaching has rewards:

'It's the heat,' I said.

'I see, I get it!' said the boy. Learning is possession. It was a simple thing, and a huge lesson. It was his.

Have you ever done the Luscher Colour Test? It proves uncannily accurate. You have to select a series of colour sheets in order of preference. Then you look up a lot of stuff and it tells you a few home truths. I picked vermilion, creamy white and charcoal grey. It said I cope with anxiety by means of hectic intensity. It can say that again. In Chemistry at school we had to put red lead powder on a brick of charcoal and blow through it. This produces a blob of metal. I loved that.

Let's hear it for black and white, from Hitchcock to Bewick. I love etching and wood engraving (if you are feeling sad try F.L. Griggs). The critics say 'colour' but they mean the riches of tone, depth, sparkle and pattern. Once I booked to see the Samuel Palmer drawings in the Ashmolean in Oxford. I gazed closely at these small marvels – so vulnerable – one furious demented scrunch… With Palmer I went through the gate, passing the full stooks, the sheep heavy with fleece, up the round hill, to the moon. Then I worked out what the man did – with his pen that day in the turn of the nineteenth century.

In Patrick White's novel *Riders in the Chariot* there is a character called Himmelfarb – Heaven Colour. Does this mean pure sky blue? Or the level light, just on the edge of evening, that has been thought to be the light of heaven? This is best seen in Bellini's *Allegory of Paradise*. Some people don't care for the one light, or for 'no more sea'. Once a lady spoke to our group who had become neo-pagan. She hadn't been happy in her cradle religion, the Salvation Army, which seems a bit like Mrs Whitehouse's Festival of Light. Our lady liked the night. She was happy with a more holistic scheme.

Chromaticism in music (an analogy) means that the scale mounts by means of short intervals, as the rainbow proceeds. Colour, of course, is not a thing. It is the way we perceive different wave lengths of light. The Structuralist writer Claude

Lévi-Strauss[33] thought that chromatic music as in Wagner's *Tristan und Isolde* was very suitable for the theme of adultery, because it bridges the space between marriage and not-marriage (some deplore the whole package).

When they told me I had ARMD (Age-Related Macular Degeneration), I read 'avoid blue'. Must I really give up Bristol glass, my domed kitchen lamp that looks like lapis-lazuli, morning glories, lapis-lazuli...? It seems not. I can keep my blue curtains. It is actual blue light I must avoid. 'Try reading with yellow lenses.' When art people say 'colour' they mean colour dynamic, what one colour does to another. It's as if Vermeer says, 'No yellow without blue.'

Last September (in full possession) I was reading, on the bus to Oxford, a review of an art installation. The people had found a squalid old flat or hovel somewhere in London. They poured copper sulphate into it and sealed it. Time passed and everything, rotten doors, old bath, became transformed by those blue gems. Later at the Conference we heard it described by the critic Jonathan Jones. 'Redemptive,' he said. It evidently redeemed the space. I keep forgetting that I haven't actually seen the thing.

In the dim light of the newly-furbished museum in Leeds, I could just pick out the blue faience Egyptian beads. Now my tulips are out, no blue in sight, but other things are blue. Is blue simply worth living for? (One silly blue plastic tulip amongst my yellow ones in a vase, rather suggests that it may be – in passing.)

At Christmas, before the trauma, I admired the kitchen jar full of plastic implements in brilliant colours. 'Dost think,' says Toby to Malvolio, 'that because thou art virtuous we shall have no more cakes and ale?'[34] Or , in my case, no more coral pink spatulas, turquoise blue bowls and a sort of lemon coloured whisk... Does anybody know where I can buy a marigold orange anglepoise lamp?

---

33 Claude Lévi-Strauss, *The Raw and the Cooked*, translated by John and Doreen Weightmann (Jonathon Cape, London 1969).
34 *Twelfth Night:* IV:3.

Real Teachers Want to Explore

Alison McRobb

Scripture, Bible Knowledge, Religious Instruction, Knowledge, Education, Studies ... the progression of names for the subject during my four decades in English schools is significant in itself. Apart from some time-out in the 1980s when pressed by a flattering number of local parents in Cambridge to teach their children, and sometimes themselves, to love playing the piano and the clarinet – and a short period of 'over-qualified' joblessness following a year of advanced professional study, when I fell back on charring – I've been swept along in the development of RI, RK, RE, RS, always somehow entangled with the Fourth R.

My year at Jordanhill College of Education in Glasgow, 1965-66, was one turning-point: a surprised introduction to a 'new' subject. At Kilmarnock Academy, where Classics in the 1950s retained its traditional supremacy, 'Bible' had been for pupils a dreary single period of reading passages, mainly Old Testament, around the class – followed by 'gym' , but only on *wet* days when a double period at the games field was impossible! Occasionally the formidable Miss Cameron, who had taught my father in the same classrooms, would comment tersely in her precise Highlands and Islands delivery. At other times she nodded off. We sat quiet till our verse came round, though there was no lesson plan, no homework, no exam. We were in awe of the lady, famous for the hand-knitted woollen stockings glimpsed beneath her stern tweeds, and for her ownership of an original Morris car, still being driven by this ancient of days.

Fast-forward to 1965 and my first RE Diploma lecture at Jordanhill with another formidable lady, Miss Mary Adam. I was an unwilling student. After four rewarding years of Honours Philosophy and English Literature at Glasgow's 'proper' (ancient) University on the banks of the Kelvin, I had expected to follow the male thinkers and read Theology over at Trinity College with its distinctive black tower. Today the same tower, cleaned up, gleams in sunshine. Then, no luck. Theology (always a second degree in those days at Scottish universities) could not be funded for students not seeking the BD for professional purposes – so, no women, at least no poor ones. Since I aimed to be a teacher, well anything but a cleric, I was scuppered. 'Bible' had become 'Religious Education' even in Scotland, but a theology *degree* was not required. So I sat grumpily among a dozen chaps, all, for some mysterious reason, ex-clerics of the Presbyterian persuasion, while Miss Adam faced us with the task of introducing Mark's Gospel to 13-year-olds. 'What,' she asked, 'would you tell a class about this author? Who did Mark think Jesus was?' 'The Son of God,' ventured one of the Revs. She wrote that on the blackboard and looked at me. 'A man worth writing about,' said the bolshie one. Mary wrote that down too, with a wicked smile. 'Well, we've got the whole range of possibilities here,' she began. We're still friends. Quite recently I discovered that she had got the RE lectureship out of a strong field of a dozen candidates – and her discipline had been Chemistry, not Theology. Times certainly were a-changing.

Let loose on the world of work, and landing – via fate and marriage – south of the Border, in the same sacred space as the likes of Nineham and Moule, I proceeded to teach what had become RE, and in the process taught myself some theology. For 'theology' of course read 'Christian theology.' A few services in the awesome presence of Hugh Montefiore at Great St Mary's, Cambridge's University Church, ensured that our family would be an Anglican one, with Presbyterianism swiftly lapsing into hazy memory, even for my son-of-the-manse spouse. Cambridge, however, was also the home of the 'Local' Examinations Syndicate, and by the early 1970s I was beginning my parallel career as an RE examiner, scooping a first Chief Examiner post in 1976. A young Don Cupitt, who appeared at several 'syllabus development' meetings during this period, was always entertaining company, asking, as I still think, all the right questions. Rubbing shoulders with the 'gentlemen' theologians from the Faculty, who had the vacation time, and the sense of responsibility, to run the Cambridge school examinations in those days, gave me *carte blanche* to be as radical as I liked, more than making up for the lack of a traditional theological education. Never once did they look down on a 'mere' school-teacher. Everyone's ideas were treated with respect. Nothing as revolutionary as 'other religions' had as yet been mooted at A-Level, but I was quick off the mark when I found that my preferred field of Ethics was to feature in an up-dated Cambridge A-Level paper entitled 'Principles of Christian Belief and Action'. This was a breath of fresh air after the strictures of 'Prophets' and 'Gospels'. I was appointed Chief Examiner and watched the clientele grow from a few hundred to thousands in the 1990s.

So where had 'radical' entered the picture? Can one be born that way? Learning to be a person without a father – he soaking up sunshine with the RAF in India till I was almost 4 years old – I must have taken my cue from the independent minds of a houseful of wartime women, particularly two talented aunts. The elder – like me a redhead, writer and teacher, unlike me an extrovert raconteuse and comedienne – let me play with her infant class's pictures and words on flash cards. Soon I was reading. The other, a former art student from the hallowed realms of Rennie Mackintosh, got me painting. Everyone could sing and recite yards of poetry: aunts, Mum, and especially Granny. Bedtime prayers were said, church no doubt attended, but religion didn't get heavy till we re-located post-war to the Village. By then the honeymoon period with my film-star-looks father in uniform was over. I was noted to be an asker of unwelcome questions, a sceptical examiner of sacred truths and a digger-in of heels when Authority dictated the (to me) illogical. Proper parents like mine were expected to see that, for their own good, awkward, argumentative children were not given an easy time. They did their duty. As for church in the village, even for my fairly liberal parents, this was Presbyterianism at its heaviest. We all did our duty: two services each Sunday plus Sunday School. In lengthy sermons, Death got a much higher profile than Life. I argued, wept, worried, once fainted in church, even, at 9 years old, lost a patch of hair – at which point things did get a little less heavy.

The nice village school presented no challenges, but Secondary School in town was bliss. Literature was a free for all (never any 'set' books). Languages: I was revelling in French, Latin and Greek by the age of 12. If you had ideas you were not slapped down. Strangely, however, I was encouraged to explore ideas without learning, until I reached university, that there was a discipline called Philosophy. I joined the Scripture Union, played the piano for 'choruses' and sizzled sausages with them, but firmly declined an invitation to 'give my testimony'. On a hike to Ben Lomond I read the entire Fourth Gospel in booklet form presented by an older girl. I asked why it was so totally different from the other three. 'He was an old man by that time,' she said confidently. 'He'd forgotten the details.' I was unconvinced. Later I sat in the school dining room sneaking a first look at the pristine green hardback newly published NEB[35] New Testament I'd just spent pocket money on. But would my parents be equally impressed?

Once I discovered what Philosophy was, it seemed obvious that I should leave Anglo-Saxon to others, keep the Eng. Lit and do a double degree. Philosophy meant thinking things out – which I did from dawn to dusk anyway. A first-year subsidiary class, an innovative stab at Religious Studies in an Arts Faculty, was an eye-opener, however. I did badly at first, getting slated for my 'literary' essays, replete with G.M. Hopkins quotations, and my 'devotional' tone. But by the end of the year I had read Tillich, heard McQuarrie, and studied Romans in Greek. I was freed to think the unthinkable about the Atonement, well about everything really.

---

35 New English Bible.

People who find themselves in SOF often describe the process by which their take on things was radically changed by some Damascus experience or other. I'm from the minority who feel that they've thought something like 'non-realist' from the beginning. Not even at my most devout could I take final refuge in the seemingly illogical. The more I was given my say as an independent adult, the less patience I had with the get-out clauses of popular theodicy: that God sees the bigger picture, that all mysteries will be revealed in His good time, that foolishness is true wisdom. If it is, why should we bother to think at all? Later Buddhism presented itself as a possible escape route, and a reasonable one, but at the edges it failed to satisfy. I did spend one wonderful Christmas morning reading *Solar Ethics*[36] all the way through while the turkey was in the oven. But I'd always thought like that anyway, so it was no more shocking to the psyche than *Honest to God*[37] had been, or *The Myth of God Incarnate*[38] for that matter.

How, in that case, could I have been a happy Head of Religious Studies for so many years in every kind of school? No parental complaints? No grovelling to the Governors? No sacking? No burning at the stake? All I can say is that those were other days, before paranoia was added to the water. In my first week as a head of department I complimented a girl on her thoughtful essay, the only one of real quality in that fourth form class's first homework for me. There was a buzz of incredulity in the room. Later it was explained to me: she came from an eminent Cambridge family of academics, but had always had bad marks for RE because she, like them, was an atheist!

In the mid-1980s Fr Timothy Wright, who later became Abbot of Ampleforth, inspired development of a new suite of A-Level Religious Studies papers. (This was during six years when I

---

36 Don Cupitt, *Solar Ethics* (SCM Press, London 1995).
37 John A. T. Robinson, *Honest To God* (SCM Press, London 1963).
38 John Hick, ed., *The Myth of God Incarnate* (SCM Press, London 1977).

worked full-time as an Examinations Officer, responsible for all of the Cambridge Board's Religious Studies exams at every level, home and overseas.) Stephen Blunden, my colleague at the Examinations Syndicate, himself a theologian, thought it would be possible to produce something modern, but particularly acceptable to Catholic schools in terms of history and doctrine. For this venture we founded the Christian Theology Trust, later a registered charity, with the aim of providing materials and support for teachers, and lectures by eminent theologians for sixth-form students. The then Archbishop of Canterbury and Cardinal Archbishop of Westminster were happy to be patrons. Rowan Williams was among the first lecturers. I set the three Ethics papers in the suite of twelve modular papers.

Getting the new syllabus accepted by the quango then in power was tricky. Though squeaky clean as an 'ecumenical' not a 'Catholic' syllabus, it had one serious flaw in the eyes of the committee: there were no papers on 'other religions'. In vain did I plead that those were by now widely available in the existing Religious Studies syllabus of all the English and Welsh exam boards. One or two people round the table were obviously prepared to hate our submission in any case. Finally the new syllabus was accepted, but 'punished' in a way which was expected to give it the kiss of death in state schools at least: it was to be named not 'Theology' but 'Christian Theology.' I also had to plead with the current powers on the Cambridge Board to accept the modular syllabus. Rather rashly I had predicted that 'Theology' would become the market leader within a year or two. Actually it achieved this in 18 months, and stayed there until axed.

'Modular' is now a dirty word in education journalists' vocabulary and reviled as 'bite-size chunks you can re-sit time and again'. The Trust was wound up a few years ago when RS syllabuses were once more revised. But we Trustees had no evidence that the modular system did anything but good. It certainly encouraged hordes of 'ordinary' students to tackle important philosophical topics, which had long been only raised for a few, and then only at University level. Now school students were introduced to critical thinking and encouraged to use it themselves. RS was no longer a 'girly subject' or even a 'Cinderella subject'. Conferences and magazines raised its profile. I had taught the importance of clear, independent thinking based on reading and evidence in both grammar and comprehensive schools from the beginning. But the exam changes were radical, for teachers especially, and many were grateful for the Trust's support.

Satisfying as administrative work and development work could be, I soon gravitated back to the classroom, in this case a superb classroom in a highly motivated independent London setting: an invitation too good to refuse. You got boys at 10 or 11 years. You got a chance to explore ideas in depth. You turned out Oxbridge stars and some who were not, but left school reflective human beings on the basis of some of the seeds you had planted. The ethnic mix caused no problems in Theology class – every tradition got impartial treatment: that was understood.

It couldn't last of course. The Christian Union, quiescent for some years, was becoming more strident. Some evangelical parents were obviously enquiring over dinner as to the RS department's views on controversial topics. Students who wanted to wind a teacher up were primed with deliberately challenging questions. What in the past could have been an honest answer became perforce a carefully worded statement, steering anxiously away from any language which could be used against one in the future. Some high profile cases in the national news revealed doctrinal issues as a potential minefield, likely to land liberal teachers of the past three decades up to their necks in something unpleasant. No Muslims were removed from my department's classes on religious grounds, ever – but one devout sixth-former began to grow his beard and we could do nothing to protect him. Events took their course.

I left school teaching, therefore, a few years earlier than I might have, out of cowardice I suppose, but also because it's not good to go out on an unpleasant note. I left while it was still possible to discuss a whole world of ideas with our A-Level theology classes and get down on the floor to do Meditation, our General Studies afternoon activity, with orange-clad Sri Lankan monks or earnest Sai Baba devotees. I left while most colleagues could be trusted to respect one another's professionalism and academic respectability. Mine did, even if they thought some of the RS department's ideas to be rather loopy or, more commonly, 'too deep for me.'

In a vastly more dangerous academic world SOF has been a refuge for hard-pressed teachers as well as for 'doubting' clerics. It's not usually a matter simply of people 'losing their faith' or finding it impossible to go along with awful morning assemblies or 'realist' expectations. Real teachers want to explore all that's there, without watching their backs, without being fettered by bland 'schedules of work', pre-digested lessons with predicted 'outcomes' and vague 'moral values'. I was privileged to have followed my teaching and examining career in a golden age of academic freedom. But freedom is risky and nothing, but nothing, is allowed in education today unless it has been tested and guaranteed as risk-free. Watch this space? We might have to watch it for a long time to come.

St Matthew's Life of Jesus

Wendy Funnell

Because St. Matthew's Gospel is written as prose, the tendency is to read it as philosophy/science/history in the Enlightenment manner. I suggest that 'St Matthew' has to be considered as a dramatist and that his purpose is not to set out the Jesus who was born, who suffered and who died, as a modern historian would, but what Jesus was about, which requires a broader form. So it has been a relief to find that current critical reading of the Gospels is in favour of 'narrative criticism' and 'reader-response' readings, which is where I would locate my own approach.

Assuming some kind of integrity in the text, there is in the Gospel a problem/answer scenario but it is set out within literary, artistic parameters. Within these 'St Matthew' sets out his own problems and sorts them out within his own terms of reference. For example, he wishes to include the phrase from *Isaiah* (7:14) *'Immanuel, God with us'* into his text as part of his characterisation of Jesus. So as a dramatist, he sets it in the Virgin Birth scenario:

> Now all this was done, that it might be fulfilled which was spoken of the Lord by the prophet, saying, Behold, a virgin shall be with child and shall bring forth a son, and they shall call his name Immanuel, which being interpreted is, God with us. (1:22-23)

St. John, in my imagination, would have read this and wondered why did 'St Matthew' bother; all he had to write was *'The Word became flesh and dwelt among us';* but that is not 'St Matthew's' way. One might argue that the Word became flesh only in chapter 16: 13-18 with Peter's pivotal phrase *'Thou art the Christ'*.

And, having set up the Immanuel notion, 'St Matthew' has to establish its relevance. Hence it appears in the last phrases of the Gospel, 28:19, where 'Jesus' says, *'I am with you always'*. But 'St

Matthew' also has to make explicit the inherent notions. These are set out in the Temptations (4:1-11), as I shall shortly show, where Jesus' replies hold the line against the wrong answers being presented to the right questions. The terms are reset in 28:19-20 as he steps across the line, with the right answers.

The 'Immanuel' phrase recalls *Isaiah's* verse (7:14):

> Therefore the Lord himself shall give you a sign: Behold, a virgin shall conceive, and bear a son, and shall call his name Immanuel.

but 28:19-20 also recalls *Deuteronomy* 1:21:

> Behold, the Lord thy God hath set the land before thee: go up and possess it, as the Lord God of your fathers hath said unto thee; fear not neither be discouraged.

and *Joshua* 1:09.

> Have not I commanded thee? Be strong and of a good courage; be not afraid, neither be thou dismayed, for the Lord thy God is with thee whithersoever thou goest.

This is not 'St Matthew' marking off the tickboxes to show Jesus was the Messiah, but he is finding in the Old Testament tradition a means of understanding what Jesus was all about and also claiming that the vision which had driven the Jewish people over 1000 years or more had now become visible. *Matthew* 28:19-20 is, therefore, a masterpiece of compression in completing 'St Matthew's' terms of reference.

> All power is given unto me in heaven and in Earth. Go ye therefore, and teach all nations, baptising them in the name of the Father, and of the Son and of the Holy Ghost: teaching them to observe all things whatsoever I have commanded you: and lo, I am with you always even unto the end of the world.

It shows not only the takeover of JHVH's commissioning of the Israelites in *Deut.*1:21 and *Joshua* 1:09 but also the 'Immanuel' phrase of *Matthew* 1:22-23 now in Jesus' own name, and furthermore, the resolution of the three problems of the Temptations. Believing that the guide-lines are set out in The Temptations and their resolution in 28:19-20, I take as my basis that Jesus is not so much concerned with 'self' as with 'subjectivity' i.e. taking control of ourselves and the situation in some way. But subjectivity also includes consciousness.

1. Stones into Bread/I am with you always
'If thou be the Son of God, command that these stones be made bread' (4:3):

Is it OK to be me? The bread that Jesus liked was yeasty, leavened bread. We are not objects, but subjects. Subjectivity means taking responsibility for one's views and actions, taking the leap of courage. It's the problem of self-consciousness in the presence of the other from the Garden of Eden on. Jesus' answer is 'yes', within the context of the indwelling Christ/Holy Spirit, Abba Father as was. The Spirit becomes the context wherein we can cope with ourselves, for starters. As Psalm 69:5 has it, *'thou knowest our foolishness and our sins are not hid from thee'*. We can tolerate ourselves and live with ourselves and accept that all the voices on the internal radio are our own, both good and bad.

2. Jumping off the Temple wall/Go and teach and preach
'If thou be the Son of God, cast thyself down' (4:6):

Are other people OK? In the context of the Spirit we can grant you subjecthood also, i.e. realising that what you present me with are not your problems but your answers, and so achieve a subject to subject relationship. The 'what it is like to be me' aspect of consciousness (and which materialistic and mechanistic explanations of consciousness do not address) is a basis for our understanding of and sympathy with others and reciprocity therewith. Tolerating both ourselves and other people is enabled through 'living in the spirit'.

3. All the cities of the world/all power is given unto me
'And the devil taketh him up into an exceeding high mountain and sheweth him all the kingdoms of the world and the glory of them; and saith unto him, All these things will I give thee, if thou wilt fall down and worship me.'
(4:8-9):

Is it OK to be human? What a daft question! There's no choice. How can we answer it? Maybe the question is how are we to take ownership of our humanity, give ourselves permission to be human. To answer this fundamental existential question, without which we are concerned with little more than fashionable morality, requires an understanding of the meaning of the Resurrection, and therefore an understanding of the miracles as a whole.

It is my basic contention that there is no God who intervenes in the objective world to do such things as the miracles, let alone the Resurrection as the greatest of them all. I believe a coherent approach to them is possible, which will include the Resurrection. It is the materiality of the miracles which we try to explain in scientific terms. If we can do so it's no miracle, if we can't then it is nonsense. Against this, my method of understanding 'St Matthew' is that he uses God language and/or the phenomena of the natural world to describe mentalist states. For example, the miracles concerning the disciples show a presentation of their reaction to Jesus, which is usually one of incomprehension and confusion. Hence the storm descriptions when they are in a boat with Jesus, that is, get close-up and personal.

This is both in regard to the disciples and to the sufferers involved in their miracles. The materiality of the miracles can be a visual statement of the verbal message, in the manner of a TV commercial and the punchline. For example, in the story of the Gadarene swine (8:28-34), the afflicted is bright enough to ask, in effect, how is he to *know* he is cured – answer, by *seeing* the swine rushing over the cliff edge taking, it is presumed, the demons with them.

It is to be noted that in the Resurrection story in 'St Matthew's' Gospel, 'God' plays no part. 'Jesus' does it himself. Angels, in this Gospel, are present to people only in abnormal or shocked states of mind, as one would expect those closest to him to be post-crucifixion, and this gives the context for the encounter at the Tomb with the Risen Lord. But if Jesus is dead, for all that he leaves an enlivening presence to the disciples, where and what is the cosmic, religious significance? Caiaphas (26:65) declared Jesus' claim was blasphemy, which moves it onto a higher plane. Jesus was concerned in his natural life with the representation of 'Abba Father'. But in his death he dies the death of God and breaks the link between the Creator interventionist God of the Old Testament and 'Abba Father', while yet maintaining faith in his own vision. And so, in the Resurrection accounts, by having lost the particularity of the body, his representation of 'Abba Father' and that unique relationship, is now universalised as the Holy Spirit. At last, the disciples in seeing the 'Risen Jesus' can see what he means when the Word stops being flesh and becomes understanding and inspiration. This generalising of the message is visualised at the onset of the final act of the drama in the Last Supper, where the broken bread represents the diversity and the cup the unity of those participating in the New Covenant, prophesied by Jeremiah:

Behold the days come, saith the Lord, that I will make a new covenant with the house of Israel and with the house of Judah. (*Jer.* 31:31).

The Holy Spirit brings us to be the person we are when we are loved and loving. It is intended to give that sort of confidence. This is how I read the miracle of the feeding of the Five Thousand *'and women and children beside'* (14.13-21), where Jesus' tear and share gives permission and context for generosity of thought and deed to others.

In the Spirit, with the indwelling Christ, we do not have to try to achieve an impossible 'goodness', but accept both our individual failures and successes, and the aspirations and limitations of humanity as such. The realisation that we are loved, despite our vices and not because of our virtues, could be seen as sharing the same values as the doctrine of *Justification by grace through faith*. In short we can have an understanding of ourselves as 'good', not just moral rule-book goodness but of value. We do not have to look around at our fellow-humanity and be reminded that we are 'fallen', that is, second class. So it does answer the question *how* as well as *why* we can believe ourselves to be 'good'. It is OK to be human. It is OK to be us.

Jesus, as 'Son of God' gives a definition of Spirit, as where our ideas of Love, Mercy and Imagination are held. But Jesus does not so much represent archetypal human nature as the environment in which human nature can flourish. Spirit, as attitude, disposition or state, gives context for the outreach of consciousness, *consciousness of,* ourselves, others, the world at large; indeed, not just consciousness *of* but consciousness *of… as…*

So perhaps I can give myself grudging permission to believe, in my own way, in 'the love of God usward', 'the indwelling Christ', 'living in the Spirit'; even perhaps to begin to explore the 'what it is like to be' of these inspirational ideas for which the arts of the Church, even the theatre in the round of a Quaker meeting, give lift-off. If so, that's the connection I, as a child of the Enlightenment, was seeking at the beginning. To quote the Psalmist again (85:10) for a more poetic phrasing: *'Mercy and Truth have met together; Righteousness and Peace have kissed each other'.*

In Praise of SOF's Stated Purpose

John Challenor

I joined the SOF Network in 1990, as soon as I first heard of it, which was through a notice in *The Tablet,* put in by Ronald Pearse. This spoke of a group exploring religious faith as a human creation, and of a summer conference.

I had spent nearly twenty years as a Roman Catholic priest, mostly in teaching, and biblical study. I had been sorely disappointed when Pope John XXIII's revolution in the sixties had been largely aborted. I had dropped out as a priest, married in an Anglican church, and remained in some sense 'religious'. I knew of Don Cupitt through his books and the 1984 TV event, and admired his willingness to argue the case for change. For me, SOF offered a new way of being religious, without having to stand apart from secular and scientific learning and defy the outside world. In terms of my Catholic past, SOF was a way out of the ghetto, and an escape from clericalism.

That was then. Now, twenty years later, how does it look? I think the aim of understanding religious faith as a human creation has proved wise, useful, and durable. It is a theory that fits the evidence. God may or may not exist, in the sense intended by those slogans on London buses: the evidence is not compelling. But in our everyday experience we can see that religious belief can be very real, and have very real effects. In the psychological order, God certainly exists. The special value of SOF is that it moves the reality of God and religion away from the metaphysical-ontological order, and into the psychological – into the human mind and heart. This is not a difficult theory to accept – it is the explanation Christians have long given for other religions and mythologies, present and past. It is the explanation already adopted by probably large numbers of our contemporaries who have arrived at it by intuition without making any long journey.

A problem arises, of course. How serious can religion be, if we treat God as constructed by the human imagination – as, to put it bluntly, imaginary? But how serious was religion in the past, when the metaphysical reality of God was taken for granted, along with belief in a supernatural revelation from outside this world? The record is very mixed. And another field of human creation – art (poetry, music, painting, the novel...) – is taken entirely seriously. (And even sport. And money too.)

Treating religious faith as a human creation allows us to make sense of the phenomena. It also frees us to jettison obsolete baggage, look afresh at the signs of the times, and speculate about the way ahead through a new agenda. For instance, Don Cupitt may well be right in arguing (in *The Meaning of the West*[39]) that the gospel, or Kingdom-Christianity, is inculturated, diffused, in the culture of Western Europe, and that Church-Christianity is dead. But if Christianity is to survive and continue, it is going to need study, initiation, promulgation, to keep it alive. In other words, there is a rôle for a church of some sort in the future, to cultivate theological understanding of our historical roots and to devise ways of practising religion in social and public life.

---

39 Don Cupitt, *The Meaning of the West* (SCM Press, London 2008).

Atheist Priest

David Paterson

'Atheist Priests' was a jeer inflicted on us in 1987 when a small group, mostly Church of England clergy, helped to found the Sea of Faith Network. We were asked 'Why do you go on being a Vicar when you don't believe in God?' Now, 22 years on, I find that I want to accept the label. But now, as then, I want to make clear what I think it means.

I'm retired now – that is, retired from being the Vicar of Saint Peter's Loughborough – but, as soon as I moved down to Oxford I knew that I wanted to be as much a part of a worshipping Christian community as I had ever been, and as much part of the priestly leadership as well. No doubt about the 'Priest' bit, then!

I was lucky to find a church which was very welcoming and open, to find how much I was able to contribute and to know the warmth of being accepted. The church is a liberal Anglo-Catholic Parish Church in Oxford, Saint Michael and All Angels, New Marston, Vicar Elaine Bardwell. When I was a Vicar I had a lot of authority and freedom granted to me by the way the Church of England manages these things. As a retired priest who is merely 'helping out', all that has gone. Or has it? I think that having to live, speak and act in a way which can inspire respect is a superb discipline. I now have no second-hand authority, granted to me by an institution, but the humbling sort which so obviously depends on how much I respect others and deserve their respect. I learnt a lot *being* a Vicar, and now even more serving *under* one. So I'm a Priest – by inclination and by enthusiasm; not just by some words pronounced over me by ecclesiastical authority, though I owe gratitude and loyalty to that authority, on which even the concept of priesthood depends.

But what about 'atheist'? To start exploring that, I go back to my first time in Oxford – as a student in 1951. I was reading Science and Mathematics, and I was a practising Anglican and a devotee of Saint Francis of Assisi. I had no doubts about evolution. Darwin had obviously made a good job of diagnosing the problem of how to make sense of such a proliferation of different forms of life, and – good scientist as he was – had set out to find an answer by research, enquiry and the accumulation of evidence. The evidence – for me – was totally convincing.

I was also fascinated by astronomy and the origin of the Universe. I favoured Fred Hoyle's theory of continuous creation and only accepted the 'Big Bang' reluctantly, as it proved to be such a powerful tool in linking a wide range of evidence. Scientific theories can be tested for accuracy in their conformity with the facts, and their usefulness. I thought the idea of an external 'Creator' unhelpful. It did nothing to explain the phenomena we experience around us, and of which we are part. For one thing, the 'existence' – in the same sense as we would speak of any object as 'existing' – of such a Creator merely adds a new 'thing' equally in need of explanation. And this new 'thing' is infinite and eternal! How do you explain that? Children are so wise when they ask 'Who made God?' So as well as St Francis and Darwin I thought very highly of the atheist authors of the time, and especially Julian Huxley. His *Religion without Revelation*[40] was a big influence on my thinking. And that rather delicious cocktail was why I offered myself for ordination in the Church of England.

I realised later that I had to be careful about the term 'atheist', and also about how I answered the question 'Do you believe in God?' St Francis believed deeply in God. He loved God, learned from God, worshipped God. And I could say yes to all those things; I saw the point of them and wanted to do them better. Francis saw the whole of the natural world as God's Creation, and therefore so did I. But the significance of it for me was

---

40 Julian Huxley, *Religion without Revelation* was first published in 1927.

experiential, emotional, practical, spiritual and mythical – not pseudo-scientific (and I think Francis, within the thought forms of his time, was not very different). God 'exists' – if you really want to use that word – as an idea which expresses itself as an ideal, an attitude, a commitment, and above all a sense of wonder. 'God' is totally unnecessary as an *explanation* of the world, but a wonderful aid to understanding our place in it.

'Do you believe in God?' – 'With all my heart and mind and strength.'

'Do you think God exists?' – 'No, I don't think the question even makes sense.'

What is a Priest anyway? There are many very diverse answers to that; but, for me, when I became a Vicar in Loughborough, it was about leading a Christian community which would care for the people who lived in their parish. One of the big problems at that time was homelessness, and we did a great deal of work housing people – in the Vicarage, the Community Centre and the church building itself, and over the years we helped to open and run four hostels.

At the same time, migrants and refugees were arriving in Loughborough from Bangladesh, Panjab and East Africa – Muslims, Hindus and Sikhs. This became a local issue. Some people were afraid, and for most it was at least an unsettling experience. Racial prejudice was a growing danger, and the churches weren't always free from it. Loughborough hadn't had an Afro-Caribbean influx in the 1960s, so this was a new experience. The humanitarian task was to make the immigrants feel welcome, and for me this was therefore part of the job of the Vicar, part of the priestly rôle. The task of welcoming these strangers into what was too often a hostile climate was tackled by many people, mostly to the left in politics or the liberal side of Christianity. It was a good combination. Co-operation depended on holding on to the ideals and the purpose, and not letting the irrelevant differences get in the way. It didn't matter whether you believed in the existence of God or not, though if you'd worked with someone long enough and trusted them, it became very interesting to share these differences. It might matter too what sort of deity you did or did not believe to exist.

The incomers had some ideas and practices which seemed very strange to us. How on earth could intelligent people believe these outlandish things and perform these strange acts of worship? Respect was the essential ingredient, and then understanding could grow. We started to feel the deep spirituality in the scriptures and rituals of these other cultures, and why they were so important to our new friends.

From respect and a deepening understanding came the sharing of a large variety of religious experience. The deeper the religious experience, the less divisive the differences became, and the more interesting. Experience of the divine is essentially diverse because what is being glimpsed or attempted is a grasp on what is infinite. Our myths and the myths of others are not different in kind. It cannot be that ours are facts and theirs are human creations. A lot of inter-faith work still does make that assumption, but I can't help thinking that is toe-in-the-water stuff. I'd rather dive right in. *All* religions are human creations. *All* gods are personifications of ideals. Our own religion and our own god cannot be made an exception.

There cannot be just one way of understanding the infinity of it all. Yet in their deepest expressions, human faiths become profoundly aware of the unity of it all. In fact, that seems to be the commonest mystical experience, which in some way or another has been shared by many people – most perhaps, or even all. Some realise that such an experience makes possible an understanding of our unity with each other across all human divisions.

In 1987 lots of people who had responded to Don's television series *Sea of Faith* came to a radical Christianity conference at Loughborough University. From it the Network was born. Three months later I went to India for the first time. I went to Gujarat to see whether we could set up a link with a town in that State, and so help Loughborough's citizens – those of English descent and those of Gujarati descent – to grow in respect and understanding for each other. I was invited by an organisation which was following a Gandhian agenda in education, health care and appropriate development.

Gandhi wrote: 'Religion which takes no account of practical affairs and does not help to solve them, is no religion.'[41] Every religion the world has ever seen is essentially about a set of ideals, and those ideals may be good or bad, about love or hate, freedom or slavery. They vary in practice from depths of stupidity and cruelty to heights of wisdom, love and creativity. The test must always be the humanist one. Does this faith help people to be more richly human in wonder and worship, thought and understanding, compassion and action?

The Sea of Faith Network took as its sub-heading the phrase 'religious faith as a human creation'. The point was made by Don many times that we human beings are responsible for our religions. Humans in the culture of their times have created them, and humans in our own time and place can change them. We are responsible for testing all of this by the humanist standard of love. Does our faith set us free, or is it a trap? The idea is not absent from the New Testament (far from it) – 'The Sabbath was made for man, not man for the Sabbath' – 'You have heard that it was said…..but I tell you…' – 'The truth will set you free.' It wouldn't be hard to find similar passages in the other scriptures of the world. Perhaps we should undertake the task some time. Religion is not there to hide behind. Submission to the will of God should not be allowed to deteriorate into 'God will do it for us'. What we think our God can do is, in the long run, identical with what we ourselves can and should do. It is therefore vital to develop a god who really is good!

No one tradition has ever asked all the possible questions, let alone given all the possible answers, so multiculturalism is not

---

41 *Young India,* 7th May 1925, page 164.

only a fact of the modern world, but also to be valued in itself. There are many ways of understanding our world, and they each have their value; but none can stand alone. I think a 'religion as a human creation' stance should be a good tool to use in the present dilemma about multicultural Britain. It could underpin respect for a wide variety of traditions without letting them divide society into cultural ghettoes.

Too often multiculturalism is promoted with the vital ingredients missing – the vital ingredients of respect and dialogue. In Bhavnagar, Loughborough's link town in Gujarat, the Muslim and Hindu communities have lived side-by-side, mostly in peace, for hundreds of years; they lived separate lives of tolerance and respect. But they didn't mix. They didn't really understand each other. And when it became politically expedient for some people to cause conflict, it was all too easy to ignite an explosion of misunderstanding, fear and hatred. Any multicultural society must pay a lot of attention to avoiding that fatal mistake. For me, this is helped by acknowledging that religious beliefs and practices are not to be exclusive but inclusive, not divinely determined but of human origin, not in competition; and above all, within our control and responsibility.

In the last few years there has been a remarkable resurgence of interest in religion. Far from being in its death throes, as many Western philosophers from Nietzsche onwards have thought, religion has revealed itself again to be a major social and political influence. Mostly – it has to be said – that influence has been bad, unhealthy and dangerous. It has been about power and control, and it has been backed by exclusivist truth-claims. The Christian Right of the United States of America uses its country's immense international power – military, economic and cultural – to impose its standards on the world, and the standards seem to have more of greed and power in them than of love. The State of Israel justified its cruel oppression of the Palestinian people by Zionist interpretations of its Scriptures, ignoring humanitarian considerations, and it repeatedly responds to understandable protest with an escalation of force.

The Muslim Umma, oil-rich in some parts of the world, has spawned protest against the domination of the USA and its allies. Many of those protests we could well support in the name of justice. At least something is being done to stop the creeping subjugation of the whole planet under the hegemony of hyper-consumers out to destroy the planet for their greed. But the protests are too often in the same terms – violence in the name of one god is countered by violence in the name of another. One bigotry against another. A competition in fear, greed and hatred. And the poor and weak, as always, are those who bear the most suffering.

Not only the religions of the world, but also its political systems, must be continually tested by the humanist test of compassion. Do they help a better humanity to evolve? – a more beautiful world, a more just society, greater freedom, the flourishing of talent. Do religious communities promote wonder at our amazing universe? Do they work for peace? Or do they do nothing to stop fear, greed, slavery and misery retaining the upper hand? Are they in fact a major part of the problem?

All my life I have believed that the religions of the world hold the highest ideals that humanity has ever attained. A huge variety of them, built up age after age and in many different places. If we are prepared to use these treasures as resources for peace, which can be shared, then this is the greatest hope for the world. If they continue to be merely competitive truth-claims, the ills will be compounded.

The task of philosophers of religion should no longer be to try to find proofs of the existence of God. That is pointless. Rather it should be to understand and promote the importance of that atheist, humanitarian, secular faith which values and respects all faiths and promotes human responsibility for them. The part of the priests, pastors and ministers, imams, rabbis, pujari, monks and nuns and all other servants of their communities is to help those communities put this into practice

So I'm happy to be called an Atheist Priest, to help in the long process of restoring spiritual treasures to the people and the planet; and I believe that the Sea of Faith Network has a vital part to play in this stage of human evolution. A stage in which, perhaps for the first time, humanity is in charge, for good or ill.

Political Morality

Denis Gildea

Growing up, I had some contact with establishment religion, at school where I was confirmed as part of the syllabus, and later in the Navy. At home we knew we were supposed to go to church, but never had the time. But in 1954, when I was 30 and babies were coming, we had them baptised to be on the safe side, and then thought they had better go to church to learn some morality. I got deeper into the church, and was soon on the PCC[42] and later the diocesan conference/synod. I was enthusiastic about South Bank religion, New English Bible and modern liturgies, to make Christianity more intelligible as a basis for action. When in 1969 the General Synod, after 12 years of negotiation, rejected unity with the Methodists by a 31% minority vote. I was deeply disillusioned. If the church could not cope with reconciliation, how could it be the motive force for a better world? I got involved in founding a local ecumenical community project, but the ministers of the eight churches did not show much interest and the church connection mainly disappeared. When three years after retiring from the civil service I dropped all these activities, including the church, in 1987, I realised I had really been in it for the politics, which term for me includes all collective action by groups of people.

I joined the civil service in 1948 in the Board of Trade and spent most of my time in it under its changing names, apart from two tours in Cabinet Office. I had 17 jobs in 35 years, which reduces boredom, and half my time was in international commercial policy, my main interest since student days. In 1949-50 I had nine months in the UK Delegation to OEEC,[43] cooperating with Europe to earn the Marshal Plan dollars. We

---

42 Parochial Church Council.
43 Organisation for European Economic Co-operation.

were 'dragging our feet' when, as liberators, we could have had the leadership of Europe. In my youthful innocence I thought we could do it, if only Ernest Bevin were not Foreign Secretary. How wrong could I be! I was involved in all the attempts to get into European integration: to have a 17-country European Free Trade Area in 1957-59; to form EFTA[44] in 1959-60; to actually join the Common Market in 1961 and 1970-72.

The other issue which gave me a lot of satisfaction was that in 1962-64 I had to co-ordinate a Whitehall policy for the first United Nations Conference on Trade and Development. As always 'dragging our feet' was the natural starting position, but the result was that the Board of Trade became and remained one of the more forthcoming departments, and Edward Heath, who led our delegation in the conference which lasted three months in Geneva, got the point in a big way, so that after his fall he was a leading member of the international commission led by Willy Brandt, which produced two reports around 1980. Following the UNCTAD, I was one of three civil servants who became rather active 'observers' in a committee preparing a booklet on *World Poverty and British Responsibility* for the British Council of Churches. This led to my being on the board of Christian Aid in 1972-84.

I am rather proud of my generation in Europe (do I have to say 'including UK'?) who were of military age in the Second World War. There was an idealism inspired by a feeling of 'never again!' about wars and slumps, and of working together for fairness and social justice, which led to what Eric Hobsbawm calls 'the Golden Years'.

This started to break down during the 1970s and opened the way for the Reagan-Thatcher reforms in the 1980s for laissez-faire capitalism, according to which what we live for is to maximise profits, incomes, consumption and competitiveness. At the government level, success is measured by Economic Growth. The touching faith in the infallibility of free market forces to maximise efficiency and wealth has now suffered a crushing blow,

---

44 European Free Trade Association.

but no new principles have yet emerged. I think our morality is not what we say we aim at, but what actually governs our conduct. Perhaps collective ethos is a better phrase, since morality is almost as much a switch-off word as God. Remember the chorus of disapproval when Robin Cook mentioned an ethical foreign policy. Stick to the national interest!

At present it is still politically impossible to give up the idea of perpetual economic growth. The concept of fairness or less inequality or social justice may creep into the debate. But any effective world policy on sustainability and Global Warming is impossible if the developed world insists on ever more consumption. That is why I support the ideal of Happiness. We all want to be happy. On reflection perhaps we do not really want it to be at the expense of other people's happiness. But how to achieve it? I am a fan of Richard Layard's book *Happiness: Lessons from a New Science*.[45] It can be shown experimentally what increases or diminishes happiness. Above a certain modest level, increasing income does not increase happiness.

What about religion? It is a pity that we are still hooked on the Victorian dilemma: Does God exist? Yes or No? It begs the question: What do we mean by God? In my later days as a practising Christian I tried to define a God I could believe in: God is the Spirit of the Love of Christ, and is within and between us. The only biblical support I could find was 1 John 4:16. But it is so far from the Almighty God of the *Prayer Book*, who if we praise and flatter him correctly will fix things for us, that it did not help me much to be comfortable in the church.

I think religion has two valuable functions, morality: the art of living together, human relations; and spirituality: self-awareness and the search for inner peace. But if you look at the church, it seems that its main function is to hold church services and try to get people to come to them. Tolerance, understanding, reconciliation, cooperation, com-passion, love is a rising scale.

---

45 Richard Layard, *Happiness: Lessons from a New Science* (Penguin, London 2005).

Unity of denominations, acceptance of women and homosexuals do not inspire much enthusiasm in the church. But many of our moral ideas do come from religions at their best. I believe Karen Armstrong is trying to draft a Charter of Compassion from all the major religions she has studied. This seems valuable, at least as a way of reducing the damage religions do to each other. But in Western Europe whatever is said in the name of religion is unlikely to carry much weight. The Greatest Happiness is a more easily comprehensible objective, and can start the never-ending debate of how to achieve it. At this moment, when competitive 'selfish capitalism' has pretty well collapsed, we need another moral revolution, as in the 1940s, reversing the direction taken in the 1980s. We must find a way of living more modestly, and learning that our happiness is not achieved at the expense of others.

I will finish on a more personal note. I look rather miserable and do not socialise easily. I did not achieve the dizzy heights in my career that I fantasised about when I passed well in the entrance exam. But thanks to my wife, who is more hostile to religion but far more spiritual and sociable than I am, we brought up five children and have 17 grandchildren, and we are very proud of them. We celebrate our Diamond Wedding next year. At 85 I have had my ration, and have no desire to maximise the length of my life, but when the time comes I would hope it would be quick, and not long drawn out. My only religious activity is the annual SOF Conference. I am not hoping for any afterlife. Too much like hard work! My immortality is being remembered in the latter part of this century by my grandchildren. I wrote my memoirs in my seventies, in a typescript 'private book', which had a circulation of 25, to the extended family and a few friends. I recommend others to do it as, unexpectedly, it turned out to be therapeutic. I end with its last line: So I claim not to be depressed, but to be complacently contented.

Ecology and the Strangeness of the Present

Victor Anderson

Every generation faces its challenges – in fact 'challenges' is an extremely weak word for fighting in a World War or coping with poverty in the Great Depression. Current generations face the global ecological crisis, every bit as serious as those previous 'challenges', but for some reason we are not galvanising ourselves and we are not taking effective action, at least not yet.

Future historians are likely to look back on this as a very strange period. We have more scientific information about the state of the planet and its ecosystems than has been available at any previous time. We have found out what is going on, and we know roughly what the consequences will be if current trends continue. Yet we are hurtling towards disaster, and not only in terms of climate change, but in terms of a general degradation of the ecosystems which support and constitute life. This is a strange time to be living.

Of course many people are refusing plastic bags, changing lightbulbs, perhaps reducing their car use. These actions all contribute to a gradual cultural shift, but they tend to be tokenistic, small-scale, and simply not up to the size of the task. This crisis is a general crisis which requires a social solution. 'The environment' is, by definition, what surrounds us all. Therefore the problems can't be dealt with through individual actions, because we don't just each have our own individual separate environment. Dealing with ecological issues requires humans to act as social beings, pursuing social solutions, including the use of political action and institutions.

Since we are currently not dealing effectively with ecological issues – and the evidence for that is simply the general worsening of global ecological indicators, such as global average temperature and rate of species loss – we need to examine our social institutions and ask whether they are hindering or helping, whether they provide anything like the means of change which the ecological crisis makes necessary. People have looked from different perspectives at different institutions, and produced critiques and responses focused on just one area – the economy, religious beliefs, political system, etc. – but what exists now is a more general and systemic problem, involving all these areas in combination and synergy with each other.

An economy not grounded in its resources

The financial crisis which hit in Autumn 2008 demonstrated very clearly the failings of the current economic system. Now not only Communism has been seen to fail, but neoliberal market economics too. Neoliberalism failed to eradicate poverty, brought the world further into ecological crisis, never even attempted to move towards social justice, and constantly escalated the amount of risk in the economy. The finance sector was allowed to get away with gambling and risk-taking on what proved to be a catastrophic scale, and now taxpayers are essentially taking on debt in order to pay off the finance sector's losses.

The finance sector lost touch with reality. However this is simply the most extreme example of what has happened to the economy as a whole. The economic system depends on natural resources and the services provided by ecosystems, such as water supply and breathable air. Yet the economic signals which guide firms' behaviour do not generally take these into account, by penalising pollution, for example, and giving credit for cleaning things up. There are some taxes, penalties, and subsidies, but they are often relatively haphazard, not the result of a full-scale design of economic signals to reflect the reality of dependence on the environment.

In that sense, the way the economy works – for example, which resources the price system tells us are expensive and which it tells us are cheap – is not grounded in the realities of the resources which the economy depends on. We have a dysfunctional economy. At a national level, indicators such as Gross Domestic Product do not have anything subtracted from them to reflect resource depletion or environmental degradation. Economic growth (growth in GDP) is pursued regardless of its environmental impacts, remaining the number one priority of the economic policies of governments around the world. Economic theory has still not come to terms with ecology, which does not feature centrally in either neoclassical theory of the market, or in Keynesianism, and features only in distorted form, viewed through the neoclassical paradigm, even in the sub-discipline of 'environmental economics'.

The economy rolls on, most of the time, as though it is outside of human control. Yet it would be possible to redesign economic theory, economic policy, and the incentives which guide economic behaviour, if that is what we as human beings decided to do. We don't have to just put up with dysfunctional economics. However, doing something about that probably depends on taking action through political systems, and these are also part of the problem.

A political system not dealing with the issues

What ought to be happening in this situation is a rush of concerned citizens into the political process, trying to use political institutions to put the situation right, through taxation, international treaties, and so on. To some extent, this is happening. But the extent is limited. If you observe most political debate and news coverage, a large proportion of the time and newsprint is taken up with petty point-scoring, trivia, exaggeration of the significance of small differences between parties, gossip about personalities and celebrities, misleading spin and hype, reannouncements of 'initiatives' which have been announced before, dodgy statistics, and so on. As general elections get closer, and the opportunities for the public to be involved increase, the standard of political argument generally goes into decline.

Meanwhile, issues emerge and develop which the parties are ill-equipped to respond to, especially if they involve natural science (which most politicians know very little about) or religion (which they generally steer clear of), or anything which doesn't fit neatly into existing party ideologies (ecological issues generally fall into this category).

The British political system has some additional difficulties, which do not apply elsewhere. There are very major 'barriers to entry' (to use the term economists apply to new firms trying to get into a market dominated by existing firms). The lack of proportional representation makes it very difficult for new parties to enter the political system effectively (unless they are highly concentrated geographically). 25% of the vote spread evenly across the whole of the UK would be unlikely to win a party a single seat in Parliament.

Within parties, it is very difficult for people to emerge as leading figures unless they have first worked their way up through the existing party hierarchy. The American primary election system allows for an 'insurgent' candidate, such as Obama, to challenge the candidate of the party structure (in 2008, Hillary Clinton). There is no equivalent in Britain: insurgents do not become party leaders, because there is no innovative input from the electorate similar to that provided by the primary system.

More generally, across Western democracies, there is a problem of representation. Membership of political parties has fallen. Parties tend to be more centrally organised, the selection of candidates and the debates at party conferences more manipulated. Similarly, the larger NGOs[46] are increasingly professionalised, with members becoming simply part of the 'funding base', with the only way to participate in NGO decision-making being to join the staff.

---

46 Non-governmental organisations.

A further problem is the increasingly global nature of political issues. Democratic structures built up on a national basis have not been effectively extended to global level. The economy and ecology are global, but democracy has got left behind. There is therefore now a great distance between the reality of the issues of our time, and the forms of representation and decision-making which are supposedly there to cope with those realities.

Religious assumptions which do not serve us well

Despite its decline in parts of the West, religion remains an important force in shaping the basic assumptions of even the most 'secular' person, simply because of the impact of generations and centuries of repetition and influence. The basic problem here is dualism. Christianity absorbed the tendency in Ancient Greek thought which said that the spirit or the mind was 'higher', 'better', 'cleaner' than the body, nature, and matter. A powerful symbolism developed, in which the 'opposites' of dark and light, female and male, matter and spirit, body and mind, were all correlated. This is reflected in art, philosophy, gender, ethnicity, and everyday speech, right through to the present day. If nature is undervalued for centuries, an ecological crisis is an unsurprising result.

There has also been a tendency for religion to become privatised, so that it is about the individual, and the individual's conscience and way of life, and not about that person as a participant in the life of society. The dualism can then be extended into 'good' virtuous individual versus 'bad' outside society. This is exactly what is being reflected now in privatised responses to ecological issues: rather than act as a citizen, acting instead as an individual, so that the 'green consumer' becomes just another market segment, and religion becomes just one of the influences which might motivate someone to be a green consumer. An approach to religion which met our current situation would affirm the value of nature, matter, body, and life, and would seek to express that sense in society and politics, and not simply through individual lifestyle and private gatherings.

Losing a sense of narrative when we need it most

Galvanising ourselves to confront the crisis of life on Earth depends on being able to think long-term, to see the big picture and take action to address its major features. However it is very hard to think long-term in a cultural context in which a sense of history and future has declined. A key factor here is the problem of 'post-modernity'.

Post-modernity, as described by Jean-Francois Lyotard and other postmodernist philosophers, is about the absence of 'grand narratives'. Grand narratives gave a sense of shape, meaning, and often purpose, to historical development, providing a sense of 'Progress' for society as a whole, and to individuals within that context.

Grand narratives have come in many varieties. Some sought purpose in history through a special role for their own nation. Some saw it in Christian terms, as being about the road from the Garden of Eden, via the Fall, the Incarnation, and the Crucifixion, towards the Kingdom of God. Some thought history was about the increasing discovery of scientific knowledge, promoted and spread through education, applied through industry and technology, and resulting simultaneously in a greater understanding of truth and a higher standard of living. Others gave history a specifically Marxist shape, with different forms of class-divided society leading, through different forms of class struggle, to a classless communist future. Different versions and syntheses, and other alternative options, have been developed as well. But despite all the variety, there was essentially agreement on the most basic point of all: that it all meant something and led somewhere.

Such long-term frameworks led easily to long-term projects and decisions being generated, whether these were preparations for national ascendancy, spreading the Gospel, new scientific discoveries, or overthrowing the ruling class. Where, however, there is no sense of 'grand narratives', there is no long-term analysis and sense of responsibility to fit a decision or project into. There is only what we happen to feel like, or feel compelled to choose, at the time, and this may easily change.

The coming of post-modernity is largely a product of two developments which have affected Europe, especially in recent decades, and to some extent also many other parts of the world. These two developments are decline in Christian belief and decline in belief in Marxism. The decline in a sense of the long-term is largely an unintended consequence of both of these developments.

We are now presented with a major and fundamental difficulty. We urgently need a more long-term vision for decision-making in order to have any possibility of sensible decisions being made in response to the ecological crisis and in favour of sustainability. We are, however, in a situation where a sense of the long-term is now particularly weak, where not only has politics often contracted down into individual lifestyle choices, but where a sense of history has contracted down into today's newspapers, today's emails, and today's tasks at work.

A big agenda

The whole situation can be summed up as dysfunctional economics, dysfunctional politics, dualistic religious assumptions, and a loss of sense of the long-term. It would take a big crisis to get the world to snap out of all that. But a big crisis is exactly what is developing. The polar ice is melting now. My sense of narrative, and the lasting influence of Christianity in my head, require me to end this article with a dose of hope. My evenings spent in political meetings lead me to see this in terms of drawing up an agenda. The agenda I suggest is this:

- Rethink economic theory, to put environment and resources at the centre, and ecology and economics as a single discipline.
- Rethink economic policy to take global poverty and social justice seriously, and tackle these in conjunction with the ecological crisis.
- Rethink economic policy, designing taxes and government spending to reflect very systematically the pressures of the economy on ecology, and incentivise technological innovations which can help get us out of the current crisis.
- Seek to reform the whole political system, making it more proportional, less based on parties, and more able to deal with global, fundamental and emerging issues.
- Revitalise religion through an emphasis on its life-affirming aspects, a valuing of nature, matter, body; in some senses an 'incarnational' and 'materialist' form of spirituality.
- Establish in culture what is already established in science: a sense of 'grand narrative' grounded in the evolution of the cosmos and life on this planet, providing a powerful context for politics, economics, and our individual lives. This has been described as 'The Universe Story'.[47]

Until an agenda such as this is grasped, the current strange period in history will carry on, in which we walk in a form of sleep or hypnosis into forms of danger which we could, if we chose, avoid.

---

47 See Brian Swimme and Thomas Berry: *The Universe Story* (HarperOne, San Francisco 1992). Paperback edition published by HarperCollins in 1994.

Notes on Contributors

Victor Anderson was Environment Advisor to Ken Livingstone, and a Green Party member of the London Assembly. He recently worked as an economist for the Sustainable Development Commission, and is currently a freelance researcher on sustainability issues. **Page 150.**

Anne Ashworth's publications include her poem-sequence *The Verb To Be is Everywhere Irregular* (SOF) and her poetry-and-prose treatise *The Oblique Light: Poetry and Peak Experience* (Quaker Universalist Group). **Page 79.**

Sebastian Barker was recently appointed Royal Literary Fund Fellow at the University of Middlesex. He is a former editor of *The London Magazine*. He is married to the poet and teacher Hilary Davies. **Pages 82, 95.**

Helen Bellamy is a member of SOF and a Methodist Local Preacher. Her life in employment began at an infant school in Bradford and ended with the coordination of degree course provision in Barnsley, but it mainly involved teaching Mathematics in secondary and further education. **Page 110.**

Peter Bellenes is team vicar of Marldon and Berry Pomeroy in South Devon and serves on the Faithworkers' Branch Executive of the union Unite, and on the Council of Governors of the Devon Partnership Health Trust. He is married and is a father and grandfather. **Page 50.**

Anne Beresford lives in Suffolk. She has three children and five grandchildren. She has published thirteen poetry collections and her *Collected Poems* were published by Katabasis in 2006. **Page 101.**

John Challenor was a priest in the Birmingham Oratory. For many years he edited *Renew* (Catholics for a Changing Church). He lives in Birmingham with his wife and has a daughter, Zoe. **Page 136.**

Joanna Clark has three children, taught RE for many years, joined SOF in midlife and finally retired to enjoy freedom and grannyhood six years ago. **Page 75.**

John Theodore Cragg retired recently from his job as an escort on an Age Concern ambulance. He now does voluntary work preparing food parcels at St Mary Magdalene's Centre for Refugees and Asylum Seekers in Holloway Road, London. **Page 47.**

Don Cupitt is a fellow of Emmanuel College, Cambridge. His latest book is *Jesus and Philosophy* (SCM Press, London June 2009). He made the original *Sea of Faith* television series in 1984 and since then has written many books. **Page 5.**

Adele Davide, born in Manchester, now lives in London has published two poetry collections, *Becoming* (Migrant Press) and *The Moon's Song* (Katabasis, London 2001). **Page 96.**

Hilary Davies has published three poetry collections with Enitharmon (London) and is a former Eric Gregory award poet and Hawthornden Fellow. She is Head of Languages at St. Paul's Girls' School and married to the writer Sebastian Barker. **Page 83.**

Wendy Funnell was brought up in a Baptist Church, and attended Bible Study classes (with exams!). She later studied Philosophy and taught WEA and extra-mural courses. She has enjoyed years spent sailing in the Mediterranean and more recent travels. **Page 130.**

Denis Gildea is a retired civil servant and a long-standing member of SOF. **Page 146.**

Trevor Greenfield lives in Worthing, West Sussex, with his wife Sue, children Matthew, Kate and Freya and Molly, a three year old Labrador. He is currently the Editorial Manager for O Books Publishing House and Associate Lecturer in Religious Studies for the Open University. His book *An Introduction to Radical Theology* was published by O Books (Ropley, Hants.) in 2006. **Page 52.**

Richard Hall is an ex-Anglican priest and ex-Religious Studies/Philosophy teacher, enjoying retirement in Winsford,

Exmoor, with the Woodbees amateur dramatic society and playing banjo in the re-formed Kingston-upon-Thames Trio. **Page 67.**

Cicely Herbert is one of the trio who founded and continue to run *Poems on the Underground*. She is Arts Reviewer for *Sofia*. Her poetry collection *In Hospital* (together with the Victorian poet W.E. Henley) was published by Katabasis in 1992. **Page 17.**

John of the Cross: Spanish poet, mystic and reforming Carmelite friar (1542-1591). 'The End of the Canticle' is translated by Dinah Livingstone. **Page 94.**

Mimi Khalvati has published six poetry collections with Carcanet Press (Manchester). Her most recent, *The Meanest Flower*, was shortlisted for the TS Eliot Prize 2008. **Page 88.**

Dominic Kirkham is an interested follower of SOF and writes regularly for *Sofia*. He also often writes for *Renew* (Catholics for a Changing Church). **Page 102.**

Dinah Livingstone is the Editor of *Sofia*. Her latest poetry collection is *Kindness* (Katabasis, London 2007). She is also a translator of poetry and prose. **Page 97.**

Kathleen McPhilemy teaches English in Oxford College of Further Education. Her latest poetry collection is *The Lion in the Forest* (Katabasis, London 2004). **Page 81.**

Alison McRobb teaches theology and English Language and is a Principal Examiner in Hinduism for Cambridge International Examinations. She is a former Chair of SOF Trustees. **Page 122.**

Penny Mawdsley is a long-standing member of SOF and a former Chair of SOF Trustees. **Page 41.**

Sylvia Moody is a Classicist, psychologist and translator of Modern Greek. She is a member of the North London SOF Group. **Page 86.**

William Oxley divides his time between Devon and London, with some travelling abroad, most recently Rome and Bucharest. Rockingham Press (Ware) has just published his latest collection *Sunlight in a Champagne Glass*. **Page 84.**

David Paterson is a former Chair of SOF Trustees and the convener of the Oxford SOF Group. **Page 138.**

John Pearson lives in Newcastle upon Tyne where he teaches at Northumbria University. He is married to Pauline, and has two daughters, Jenny, 24, and Sarah, 19. He has been a member of SOF for 16 years and served in the past as both its Treasurer and Secretary. At the time of publication he is Chair of the Trustees. **Page 9.**

Daphne Rock's first collection *Waiting for Trumpets* was published by Peterloo Poets (Calstock, Cornwall) in 1998. Her last collection *Is It Now* (Hearing Eye, (London 2006) is a record of her experience at the end of life. She died in 2008. She was a lifelong Londoner, lover of cats and frogs and grandmother of eight. **Page 98.**

Tom Rubens is the author of five books of philosophy, the most recent being *Progressive Secular Society* (Imprint Academic, Exeter 2009). He has also published a selection of poems. He teaches English at Havering College in Essex. **Page 99.**

Ken Smith is Editor of SOF's internal newsletter *Portholes* and Letters Editor for *Sofia*. **Page 63.**

Bobbie Stephens Wright is a former SOF Trustee and the convener of the North East SOF Group. **Page 56.**

Anna Sutcliffe was an art teacher at various levels, latterly at Leeds Polytechnic. She has been a professional artist for 10 years. She is a long-standing member of SOF. **Page 119.**

Christopher Truman built his website: www.christophertrumanzenstructures.com for his line art. His poetry has been widely anthologised. He was born in Taiping, Malaysia and lives in Camden, London. **Page 87.**

Tony Windross is vicar of St Leonard's, Hythe. Having spent many years implacably opposed to religion, he found his way back to the Church through SOF. **Page 20.**

Helena Woddis is a relationship therapist living in Surrey. **Page 29.**

Notes on Contributors

Lynne Wycherley's latest poetry collection is *North Flight*, poems of Orkney and beyond (Shoestring Press, Nottingham 2006). A new collection *Poppy in a Storm-struck Field* (partly in memory of her mother) is due from Shoestring Press in the autumn of 2009. **Page 85.**

Acknowledgments

'End of Book' by Anne Beresford is published in her *Collected Poems* (Katabasis, London 2006).
'The Streets of La Roue' by Mimi Khalvati was first published in a Dutch translation in *Vers Brussel, Poëzie in de stad* by Het beschrijf/Uitgeverij Vrijdag (Brussels 2009).

The Editor would like to thank Alison McRobb and Mary Lloyd for reading the proofs and Oliver Essame for technical help with the SOF logo.

Note on SOF Network

SOF is a network of individuals and small groups which takes its name from the television series *Sea of Faith,* made by Don Cupitt in 1984 about the retreat of supernatural religion. SOF regards religion as a wholly human creation and a vital part of our human cultural treasury. In rejecting the supernatural, SOF is for humanity with its questing imagination and enabling dreams.

SOF Network publishes a quarterly magazine *Sofia* and a bi-monthly internal newsletter *Portholes,* which are free to members. It runs an annual national conference and local conferences from time to time. It meets in a series of local groups throughout the country.

If you would like to know more about SOF Network, join the Network or subscribe to *Sofia*, please contact:
SOF Network,
3 Belle Grove Place,
Spital Tongues,
Newcastle upon Tyne NE2 4LH
membership@sofn.org.uk
for current rates or visit the website:
www.sofn.org.uk

Copies of this book can be ordered from bookshops.
Or from the above address for £11 including postage.
Please make cheque payable to 'Sea of Faith'.

Afterword by John Bunyan

Great-Heart in the Valley of the Shadow of Death[48]

Christiana:
Many have spoken of it, but none can tell what the Valley of the Shadow of Death should mean, until they come in it themselves. The heart knows its own Bitterness, and a stranger intermeddleth not with its Joy. To be here is a fearful thing.

Great-Heart:
This is like doing business in great Waters, or like going down into the deep; this is like being in the heart of the Sea, and like going down to the bottoms of the Mountains; now it seems as if the Earth with its bars were about us for ever…

For my part, as I have told you already, I have gone often through this Valley, and have been much harder put to it than now I am, and yet you see I am alive.

---

48 *The Pilgrim's Progress,* part 2.

Index of Authors

Victor Anderson 150
Anne Ashworth 79
Sebastian Barker 82, 95
Helen Bellamy 110
Peter Bellenes 50
John Challenor 136
Joanna Clark 75
John Theodore Cragg 47
Don Cupitt 5
Adele Davide 96
Hilary Davies 83
Wendy Funnell 130
Denis Gildea 146
Trevor Greenfield 52
Richard Hall 67
Cicely Herbert 17
John of the Cross 94
Mimi Khalvati 88
Dominic Kirkham 102
Dinah Livingstone 97
Kathleen McPhilemy 81
Alison McRobb 122
Penny Mawdsley 41
Sylvia Moody 86
William Oxley 84
David Paterson 138
John Pearson 9
Daphne Rock 98
Tom Rubens 99
Ken Smith 63
Bobbie Stephens Wright 56
Anna Sutcliffe 119

Christopher Truman 87
Tony Windross 20
Helena Woddis 29
Lynne Wycherley 85